Connect with your Angels

Connect with your Angels

A Guide for Everyone

Jenny D'Angelo

Connect with Your Angels: A Guide for Everyone

ISBN: 978-1-61170-161-6

"Keeping Our Small Boat Afloat," by Robert Bly.
Reprinted from *Talking into the Ear of a Donkey*, W. W. Norton, New York, 2011.
Copyright 2011 Robert Bly. Used with his permission.

Cover: William Blake, watercolor *Christ in the sepulchre, guarded by angels* [detail].

Second Printing August 2016

Published by:

In collaboration with Andrew Harvey and

www.sacredfire.com

Sacred Fire is a media company based in Australia dedicated to authentic mystical teachings.

Printed in the USA, UK, and AU on acid-free paper.

This book in available from the co-publishers and:

amazon.com
barnesandnoble.com

With deep love and gratitude, I dedicate this book to the glorious presence and memory of Dorie D'Angelo, the first Angel Lady. She is my soul's beloved.

Together we offer it to the world.
May everyone be ever blessed by the Angels.

Together we dedicate it to all the people who know the Angels are real.

Appreciations

I would not have written this book without Andrew Harvey.
I bless him for his wisdom and the grace of his *mahavakya*.
I am honored to include one of his meditations.
For more information see www.AndrewHarvey.net

Meditation by Dorie D'Angelo used by her grace.

Author photo by Wesley Eckerman.

Ellen Farmer was responsible for Andrew's first stay in my home.
From the start, she has been unwavering in her support, steady and kind.

Friends helped me in many real ways as this book came into form.
Susan Raycraft, Pamela O'Shaughnessy, Christine Bakalis, Tilly Shaw, Georgia Kahn, Julie Rizzotto, Lauri Morgan, and Luann Robertson. I am grateful for you all.

Åke and Elisabeth Andersson supported this work and its spread in Sweden.
The Angel Circles we held there demonstrated the grace of the Angels in real life.

Love Itself is the actual form of God.
One who knows the secret of that love finds the world itself full of universal love.
~Sri Ramana Maharshi

Every day you shine out, you give that back to God.
~Rev Dorie D'Angelo

I am the Silence and the way to the silence.
I am there and the one who travels
and the road upon which those feet tread.

There is nowhere I am not.
You inhabit a space in me.
You cannot be outside me.
You are not in truth separate.
Like a leaf on the end of a liquid amber branch,
you believe you are the fluttering beauty separately.
You may think you die in that blazing crimson finery
until you waken inside me again, where you have always been.

Contents

A Welcome from the Angels

Welcome into the heart light, where we reside.
We invite you to sit with us for a minute wherever you are.
We invite you to remember how much we, your Angels, are with you and want to be near.

It is easy to slip into the warmth and comfort of the light. It is ever present. It is easy now.
Enter your heart. Feel the stillness. There between one breath and the next we meet. It is always so.

There is great light growing now in your hearts and in your world.
Welcome this new light, welcome the energy. You are quietly growing trust in yourself
as you welcome the light. In this way it is your Angels you receive.

We would like to send you messages. Easily the tender words enter you, enter your consciousness.
Such energy is grace. It helps you in so many ways: it is soothing; it is comforting; it is healing.

Call upon your Angels when you want assistance.
With loving attention, we will be with you.

Words from the First Angel Lady

You have a Guardian Angel in whose charge you were placed when you were born. Your Guardian Angel's job is to look after you alone. All your Angel needs from you to be able to help you to the utmost is recognition. Please, try talking to your Angel. If you will do this, you will have some proof within a week that your Angel is with you, ready to help you, no matter what the situation.

~Dorie D'Angelo,
Living with Angels

Preface

I would like to introduce you to the Angels, to help you awaken to their presence in your life. If 90% of people say they believe in Angels, few actually live in that belief. I know it is possible to live with the Angels, and I wish for you to know it too, for your life to include that joyous experience.

Connect with Your Angels: A Guide for Everyone presents the phenomenology of opening to the Angels. I write my story and experiences as a way of entry. You become familiar with their frequency, call it what you will—love, light, presence, radiance. It is within the pages and it carries you.

In the Angel messages, I ask for guidance about personal and mundane events as well as insights for these times of massive change. The Angels answer with inspiring and soothing wisdom. The light is woven through their words. Eloquent, accessible, filled with love—these messages are for everyone.

Andrew Harvey, the great modern mystic and Rumi explicator, ignited this project in my heart. He encouraged me throughout its writing, afforded me deep listening, insightful feedback, and structural guidance. His belief in me and in this project have taken me to a new level of trust as the Angels used me for this work. Here is part of what Andrew said:

> The quality of your writing is so beautiful. You have such a deep sense of beauty, and I want this book to reflect what the Angels have done in you. Show the progress of your soul in life to the moment when you could be transparent enough and humbled enough and both whole and damaged enough and hungry enough to be able to receive and know and be the clear, surrendered instrument of the Angels.

The text is in its present form because of Andrew. He and his visionary Institute for Sacred Activism provided its initial context. His presence in my life continues to be a boon and a flame. References to him show the power of even a few brilliant words.

Who is this book for? People who want connection with their Angels; who want calmness, peace, a feeling of comfort and support. People who know a lot about Angels and people who never thought of them as real. Here is a connection that is easy and accessible. The frequency is familiar. The benefit of communing with the Angels is the steadiness of their love. Such infinite, intimate, constant love penetrates us and we find ourselves loveable. Finally we can love ourselves. This is for everyone.

The practices in the book are simple; they can be given to anyone. Working with women on the cancer journey, I know there is no one who cannot do these practices.

Who am I to scribe this book? Dorie D'Angelo trained me and adopted me as her granddaughter/next of kin in the early 80s. Internationally known as the Angel Lady of Carmel, she was the first person to bring the angelic vibration into the mainstream. Her book, *Living with Angels*, is considered a classic in the field. Before meeting Dorie, I was international editor for Maharishi Mahesh Yogi, who brought Transcendental Meditation to the world. I am a published poet and a longtime freelance editor of spiritual texts. My life has been dedicated to direct experiences of truth and light. I receive the words from the Angels in humility, knowing them as blessings to be shared.

These pages can be read chronologically or randomly as daily meditations. We are growing in our understanding of how sacred objects such as books can be fully infused with divine energy. I believe that is the purpose and the mission of this book. The Angels say the words carry immediate blessing to the readers. I wish this for every reader with all my heart.

JENNY D'ANGELO

Section 1

My Journey to the Angels

Guidance

The Angels have said the thread of this book is guidance. How guidance, in very real ways, came to me concerning their presence. I was guided. I am guided. Opening to the Angels is natural. My teachers helped me to recognize them. Now we wish for you to know them in your life.

I will let the Angels say it, so you can read their words right from the start. You will begin to be acquainted with the gentleness and delicacy of their expression. Their words have an energetic resonance that comes out in the print. Their bliss is beyond this dimension, but the words you read are woven of their love.

My words and questions are written in one typeface. The Angel messages are presented in a different typeface to energetically mark their entry.

They ask that you read with your heart and be open to the experience of grace.

Dear One,

This narrative expresses the opening of your whole self to Divine Light and Love. This is the purpose of human incarnation in an essential way. Now that you are arriving into full consciousness, you can help in many ways. Words from the Angels are a perfect vehicle for this light to flood forth.

The purpose of this book is to help bridge the gap between daily life and what you call the spiritual realms. They are conjoining as you of humanity rise up in consciousness.

When you see us, we will be seen for our lovelight. When you—as individuals and as a collective—see and know yourselves truly as the magnificent beings you are, you will all easily recognize us as your family.

You, dear One, demonstrate someone fully legitimate in Angel communication, by your spiritual lineage. However, the real message is we are here for everyone. We have always been. Now the veils between the dimensions are very thin and diminish more every day.

We, the Angels, are the closest, most familiar, and most intimate to your personal selves. Thus we can help you precisely in the personal matters that hold you from loving yourselves. We see how it is with you.

We know you. We have been with you since your first birth. Because we are of Creator God, we have no way to judge you. We love you and assist you whenever we can. As you begin to know us and interact with us, our unconditional love for you—each one of you—begins to feel real. It penetrates you; it saturates you as you rise in awareness.

Now enough of you have reached a good level of awareness. The old third-dimensional systems of thought are clearly too thick and antiquated for these fluid times. Many of you now swim in the new water of cosmic joy and radiant awareness.

This is why we are here with you. This is what you are able to receive and transmit. Do not deny or doubt the potent service you do at this time. All is in good order to proceed.

We love you. We have always loved you.

First Sight, Early Sight

My journey to knowing the Angels. These are biographical vignettes from the beginning. Some of the names have been changed to protect privacy.

A Sunday morning. I was probably 10, my sister 12. We were just getting up, seeing what the day would bring. Mom was raging about something. I think it was a party she was going to have. I made a comment about one of the people, something that I saw.

My family knew that I saw things, but nobody paid any mind. Somehow I could hold my eyes so that I saw more. I was right most of the time, but they didn't know because they couldn't see. And I didn't say much.

My mother was particularly surly that day. I hid behind the door to our room. It gave me some sense of safety—that I could see her, I could see her coming, and she couldn't see me. She always got me and hit me anyway, but I felt excitement in the moments when I was hiding behind that door.

She grabbed me and shook me hard. Before she smacked me, she yelled in my face, "Don't you ever look like that again."

Something did freeze that day, something in me that has been struggling to emerge fully ever since. Seeing a dark cloud above someone or seeing flashes of light were common experiences for me, but I didn't know what it meant that I saw, and surely there was no one to ask. It was years before I knew.

* * * * *

In my teens I came into a period of religious fervor. Every Friday night I walked with a friend to our synagogue. The breezes of a New England twilight were soft and fragrant. Strolling along the tree-lined streets was a delicious way to end the week and come into a more sacred time. I was ready to be in the presence of the Divine. When we arrived at the small side sanctuary used in the summer, the last rays of sun were just streaming through the stained-glass windows, diamond shapes sparkling on the pews. The service was familiar, mostly in English, but the oldest prayers and blessings were in Hebrew. The ancient melodies stirred me.

The service traditionally began by lighting the Sabbath candles. "Light is the symbol of the Divine. Light is the symbol of the Divine in man." I could imagine all the women who had ever lit candles across all the ages. Then the young cantor sang the long, ancient blessing of the wine. His voice rose in clear soaring notes. Suddenly the whole room was aflame with light. Blazing light everywhere, radiating over every one and every thing. It was a kind of bliss I had not known before.

I do not remember the rest of the service or walking home with my friend. The next day I made an appointment to speak with the rabbi. Surely he could help me know what had happened. This was a symbol of the Divine I could feel.

In two days I went for my meeting. I walked into his study, this highly respected man seated at his desk, surrounded by books, photographs, and awards on the wall. I told him what my experience had been. It was thrilling to even say the words again of how it felt. I was flushed and eager for wisdom.

He leaned forward and looked at me intently. Slowly he took off his glasses. He said very clearly, "I have nothing I can say to you. I am a scholar. A rabbi is a scholar. I have no experience in what you described. I am sorry."

In my heart I did not go back. I felt so disenchanted. Light was what I cared about. It was what I was following.

In the Ashram

I had the profound good fortune to live in the ashram of Maharishi Mahesh Yogi. He was the one who brought Transcendental Meditation out into the world. He brought the whole idea of meditation out into the public discourse. I didn't quite know what meditation was, back in 1970, but life was horrible and I knew I needed something entirely different from what was going on in front of me. Kent State had just erupted. People were marching with their fists in the air. I had a rifle over my bed and I had learned to shoot. I was deeply suicidal. A friend from college had moved out to Berkeley and started to meditate. Out of a mix of urgency and desperation, I hitchhiked across country. In ten days I stood in front of her door in Berkeley, an apartment where she lived communally with other meditators. It was easy to see what a state I was in; I was lost. Something good was being offered to me. There was only saying yes.

Soon we walked the three blocks to the Berkeley TM Center, one of the first in the country. The beautiful initiation ritual and my first meditation were like gigantic peace messages from the universe. Instantly I was in a very familiar realm. My frequent childhood experience of floating high above my body and circling around, but now it was reframed within such an ancient tradition. I looked down at my hands about 40 miles below, there quietly on my lap, and I was utterly at peace. I was more relaxed in those 10 minutes than any time in the entire last year. I knew at once I would continue my practice and deepen my learning. This was the peace I wanted.

In a few months my friend and I enrolled in a six-month teacher training intensive to be held in Palma de Mallorca, Spain, and then in Fiuggi Fonte, Italy. On 1 January 1972, plane loads of young people, mostly English-speaking, arrived at the course. We were welcomed and told to begin our training by immediately going into silence for seven days. That would start things rolling. In the large, once-great hotels, each person in a separate enormous room, we did rounds all day. One round consisted of a set of yoga postures, a period of breath work, and then a long meditation. The most zealous did 16 or 17 rounds; I only ever got to 9 or 10 rounds. After the days of silence, we attended marvelous and brilliant lectures in the evenings by Maharishi. Maybe we were guinea pigs. No one knew what would happen when 2,000 people came together to meditate intensively for long periods of time. We did fasts and cleanses, we heard lectures and watched videos integrating meditation with other disciplines, but mostly we meditated. For me it was bliss. I loved the silence, the teachings, and the light.

My meditations were often filled with streams and orbs of light. Whenever I was in a period of longer meditation or in silence for a number of weeks, figures of clear light appeared to me. Lord Christ, Lord Krishna, Mother Mary. They did not speak, but they transmitted huge peace, unending love, and utter benevolence.

In June 1972 Maharishi personally made me a teacher of meditation, gave me the words "to whisper eternity" to a person. I taught for a while and then was invited to join the newly-formed university that placed meditation and the study of consciousness at the center of its academic program. It was a revolutionary idea. The first faculty members and staff were assembled at a small complex in Goleta, California, just outside Santa Barbara.

I had the staff car and was doing a final supply run because Maharishi was to be returning to the new campus that night. At dusk and directly in front of the room where the Vedic pundits were recording the entire Vedas—to be broadcast out over the Himalayas for the first time ever—another car drove into me while I was stopped at a red light. My head went through the windshield, my knees crammed against the knobs. It took 72 stitches to close up everything.

In the hospital, someone brought me audio tapes of Maharishi's lectures to listen to. She brought the transcripts as well, just to keep them together. My face was all bandaged, I could barely move. I was in some pain and was feeling quite weird, not knowing the meaning of this turn of events. My hands picked up a pencil and I began automatically to edit the pages. This was told to Maharishi. It was precisely when he had asked who would be editor for the new publications department. And so I became editor of his words. (I had a degree in English and had done advanced course work at Oxford University.)

When I came out of the hospital they wheeled me up to Maharishi in the lecture hall. He looked directly at me for a long, long time. He said it was not my fault, that very old karma had burned up in this event. A wild roar rose out of some deep place inside of me. I fell back into the wheelchair and they rolled me away. Maharishi had his cook make me some special Indian sweets.

My position grew to be International Editor for all British and American publications when I was invited to Switzerland to be part of the worldwide staff. I sat with Maharishi regularly and he trained me to think like he did. I could keep the truth of his words and the rhythm of his speech and still correct any slips that occurred between written and spoken words. After a time, I could run my hands over the lines and feel the energy in them; mistakes, breaks in thought, or typos seemed to jump off the page in different colors.

It was customary to work for six months and then take time for longer and deeper uninterrupted meditation. In all I took about two years in silence. During one such period of silence, we were in the Swiss resort town of Mürren, with views of the Eiger and Jungfrau (which I didn't see much because my eyes were closed).

It was Christmas Eve and the town was covered in deep snow and thick silence. Just when the church bells began to ring out at midnight, I saw the glorious, holy, and benevolent face of Lord Christ shine before me in my little room.

Not sad like in the churches or on the crosses, but quietly radiant with softly-glowing eyes. Only gentleness and compassion. He was shining on me, transmitting the real message of his life—love only and not suffering. I have never seen so tender a face.

During another period of extended meditation, we sat in small groups for a few hours in the afternoon. We read the entire Rig Veda out loud, taking turns reading, sutra by sutra, over and over. It was not the meaning, but the truths more ancient than the words that informed our subtle consciousness. We were to notice if a particular sutra spoke to us. A thrill rolled through me whenever one sutra was sounded:

. . . [T]he utterer of truth, radiant with truth, truth-speaking, truthful in act, speaking faith. . . .

On many occasions I saw flashes of light flickering at the edge of my vision. It wasn't until I met my beloved Dorie that I knew these orbs of light were the Angels, who had been near to me for so long.

Reeling

After living in the ashram for seven years, I came out into the world, fresh and pure and ready for life. I lived with my mother in Massachusetts for a few weeks, teaching her to meditate (the day after which she was in an unusual car accident, but she said her migraines never came back). I accepted a position in a new company starting up in Fairfield, Iowa. In the environment of the many meditators who were living there, I could feel at home in the larger world.

Within days of arriving in Iowa I met a man who was a visiting researcher at the same company. He'd never seen anybody like me—although he was older and a man of the world—and he fell in love. I didn't know exactly what this feeling was. I thought it was love. I was seeing light in everything and feeling tremendous waves of bliss. I wanted to ground these experiences in regular life.

We worked during the days and spent our evenings walking together in the small town. One night as we looked in the store windows he said, "I have no right to ask you this, but will you marry me?" I didn't know what to say. I said yes. We would be married quickly by a Justice of the Peace; we'd tell our friends and family later when we could have a big ceremony.

Unable to find a house to rent in that small town, we took it as a sign. We left the company and drove across country, back to his old stomping ground in Marin County, California. We used the last monies we had, but we were not worried. He was an early IT guy and could get work. I was used to being new in a place, I had strong feelings of guidance, and I was looking forward to living in the world with this man.

We moved into a small redwood house in San Anselmo. I unpacked boxes of kitchenware and dishes I had not seen in a decade. We set up a simple household, including a small meditation room. Each day I awoke with a heart of love and gratitude. He wanted me to meet some old friends, so we planned to invite them for a meal. In Safeway I picked out green beans, each separate one shining in the piles as if it wanted to come in my basket.

That night he slept fitfully. In the morning he walked round and round in the back yard. After some hours, I went to him and said softly, "Please, tell me what's wrong. You can tell me anything, I'm your wife." He stood stammering and then blurted out, "This is all a mistake. Goodbye."

Impossible to stay in our new house, we walked on the empty sand under the Golden Gate. He was still trying to show me how beautiful California was. He strode briskly in front of me; I averted my swollen eyes. He mumbled something about the greater courage. I watched the waves break. I picked up tiny grains of jade and bits of coral, handfuls of precious things found only on that beach. The red stones howled in my pocket.

Nobody knew we were married and already it was over. Within six weeks he left and there I was. Any sense of knowing I had was shattered and I completely crashed. I cried for hours. I cried for days. I slogged through nights of intense doubt, remorse, and shame. I was shocked and appalled at my own foolishness. What was I thinking? I had left the ashram with blessings from my teacher; things should have gone well with me. I was a naïve fool and entirely unprepared for this. I knew almost no one in America. What was I even doing in California?

I had been Maharishi's editor, yes, but when I went for job interviews, they asked, "So Jenny, what brought you to California?" Bursting out into tears is not very professional, no matter what a resume indicates. I had false starts and gnawing doubts. But I did survive and in a few years had a good circle of friends and a life that was again satisfying, if scarred. I didn't feel I was broken, but I felt I had thrown away the pure consciousness of the ashram and was not sure for what. Had I "sold a diamond for the price of spinach"?

More than ten years later this man had a dream about me. He found me and called my number, begging to come and see me. "It was the most shining dream I've ever had. It made me feel so wonderful, just like those weeks with you, which were the best I've ever known. Please let me come and see you," he begged and he pleaded. He prevailed upon me until I finally agreed. I was seeing clients by then, so I could see him like a client, just for that time. If I could see him in peace and equanimity, there would be value in it. I was ready to complete that story.

When he arrived he told me his shining dream. It was lovely and I was glad for him. The beauty of moving easily in light with full awareness can only gladden the heart. Then he told me what he'd been unable to say before. "When we were together, I want you to know that I loved you very much. When we were intimate and I touched the vastness of your life, I saw my own like an enormous black pit stretched out before me," his arms reaching out as he spoke. "There was nothing in the world that could make me jump in. Nothing. There was nothing you could have said or done." It had taken him ten years of therapy to know this and now to tell me. He hadn't meant to cause me so much anguish, didn't think it would have been so hard for me. He said he'd regret his actions till his dying day.

The marriage was a shocking piece of shadow. I only say that along with the deeper lessons learned, it got me to California.

First Meeting

I didn't even know what a healing was, I just knew I was going to see this lady. Friends of mine happened to hear about the Angel Lady of Carmel while they were making flower arrangements for a wedding. They both knew immediately that this was something they had to tell me. I knew I had to go.

When I called her number, she answered the phone, "Hello, this is Dorie speaking," in a lovely soft voice. She might have been a young woman. I said I wanted to see her and I didn't know why. "Oh that happens a lot," she said. "The Angels are arranging something, I'm sure." We made an appointment for the next Saturday, though she usually didn't see people on week-ends, she said she would see me.

I drove from Marin down the coast to reach Carmel, a charming and somewhat remote village, famous for its beauty and its creative residents. Narrow roads wound around the trees. There were no numbers or sidewalks; house were tucked under the limbs or stood in patches of flickering sunlight.

I easily found Dorie's house, turning at the statue of Father Junipero Serra. On her roof, a carved wooden sign, *Angels Landing*. Opening the gate of that white picket fence, I knew I was stepping into magic. I knocked on the door. She opened it herself. Her beautiful shining face, her wide and radiant smile, the kindest eyes smiling from beneath a nimbus of white hair. We hugged before we said a word.

In her living room, I told her about myself and my journey thus far. I had no specific ailment, but a lot of emotional pain. After a few minutes she took me into her Angel room. What beautiful stillness and peace in that small room, where she had been holding Angel sessions for so many years.

I lay on the table as she clipped a small microphone to her blouse and turned on the recorder. She placed her hands on my temples and began to speak the words to call in the Angels. "Now we join with the great healing power of the universe. We join with our own Guardian Angels, we join with the Angels of healing. This is our new friend, Jenny, and we would like for Jenny today to have a complete healing of her whole self. . . ."

Her voice was so soothing. I drifted in and out of clear awareness. I felt a deep trust envelop me, spreading into me and all around me. I sensed the circle of light energy, what I could now call Angels, around us as she spoke. Then Dorie brought in her spirit doctor, Dr. Kirk. She had told me about him, that he had been a practicing physician in Edinburgh, Scotland, in the last century. He had been working with her from the other side for many years now, and his diagnoses and light technologies were precise and powerful. Her trust in him was implicit.

Dorie's hands lay soft on my forehead as she described in detail what Dr. Kirk was doing. First he held a ball of colored light above me. It slowly revolved and splayed out streams of light in different hues, going to specific areas of my energy body. Then he put his hands on my heart and held it from the front and the back. A specific rosy-purple light emanated from his huge hands and simply cracked open this shell of a heart. In a flash all the many kinds of pain and turmoil roiled up in me, wracking me into uncontrollable sobbing. As I cried, his hands pulled out the darkness. Then he flowed in intense clear white light. After some minutes I became quiet. I felt clean and full of peace.

Dorie and the Angels took me on a journey. It was so easy to go with them, as Dorie's hands were still on my temples and her voice was the sound stream I could follow. Eventually we went to the first place of separation in my old story. Immediately after I was born I was placed in an incubator, a new invention at the time. It was a glass box with a glass top and sides, so that I could be viewed at all times. I was so tiny I could not be touched, could not be held. With Dorie now, I went inside the incubator, in which I had lain for my first three months. I saw myself, baby Jeanette, two-and-one-half pounds, aware and breathing, still part of the transcendent, hovering between death and life. With her eyes I saw the entire incubator flooded, filled end to end with Angels. "Thick as sardines," we later laughed.

There were pictures of Angels on the walls of Dorie's room. There were little statues of Angels from all over the world made from many different kinds of materials. There were books and there were songs. Now there were Angels in my heart and in my life.

Dorie later told me that she had been praying for 20 years, asking the Angels to bring someone to whom she could pass on this love and wisdom. She thought it was too late, that there wouldn't be enough time, she was already 81. She held my hands and said she knew it as soon as she saw me. I was the one she had been praying for. And she was the answer to my yearnings too. I had never seen her or heard of her before, but she was my soul's beloved. I walked straight into her heart on her doorstep.

Dorie was holding classes once a week and wanted me to come down for them. In a short time I arranged my life to do just that. Within a year I moved down to Carmel permanently. Many people loved her and wanted to do anything they could for her, so there was always somebody who had a room for me. I lived in this room or that, happy as long as I could go to her house every day.

It was a pleasure to enter her house. The old smell of lavender and rose, in the walls, in the curtains, in the rug, in the entryway. And baby powder. She used it and it lingered on the floor in her bathroom. She had a nightly ritual of olive oil, salt, and lemon juice to cleanse her skin and keep it radiant; these all scented the air. And every day she was the most loving, open-hearted, generous, and gracious being I had ever known.

At first I answered the phone and the letters we collected from the post office. We sat at her dining table and read through them. She showed me her way of writing helpful answers and healing words. We made prayer lists. I began to greet the clients and then she had me sit quietly with her when she talked with them. In the same quietness, I sat at the foot of the massage table when she spoke the healing words.

I was happy and enthusiastic every moment with Dorie. At tea time—"time for a little something"—we indulged in her favorite—International House coffees. They might have been too sweet, but she looked forward to it, so I love it too. Sitting at table, warm cups in our hands, we read *The Daily Word* from Unity Temple. If we had errands, we went to town together, we two, nearly the same height, sweeping through the streets of Carmel. We held hands, our hands exactly the same size. We were made of the same stuff. Dorie believed my strength was flowing into her and I felt her wisdom flowing into me. Every day I understood more. It was marvelous and exhilarating.

At the end of such a day, I might return to my little room, wherever it was, and cry through the night. The contrast between the mother I had—who was ashamed of all my spiritual seeking and wished I would just forget about the Angels—and this wise and radiant woman who loved me so much was cracking my heart open even more.

When I found Dorie I was forced to acknowledge whatever was not love in me. With her love around me, infusing me, nourishing me, I could go deeply into the dark sadness again. I cried for every lost, desolate moment I had ever lived. I tried to forgive everyone and myself. I had to live the truth of gratitude. I had to trust the process. It took time, grace, love, and a lot of tears.

Finally I was free from the frightening hold of despair. Dorie helped transform my heart into a place of safety. Now I knew what happiness was. I knew what happiness felt like. It was easy and light, wide and generous. I was existing on a new and brighter, lighter plane of being. The light of the Angels was informing me. My will, my wish, my desire was to give over to this, give up everything to this. I was in exactly the right place. Dorie confirmed that I had been seeing the Angels for so many years. They were guiding my life to come into wholeness.

Sight

I wanted sight more than anything. I wanted to see the Angels. When I first began working with Dorie, she made all the healing tapes. I helped the clients to relax and be more receptive to the healing. I used the Percussor on them to take off some of their more superficial tension. Dorie's cousin, Lyman, a chiropractic doctor and researcher had invented it. He was the one who taught me how to use it effectively. He said it induced alpha into the tissue. People loved it and everyone relaxed.

Dorie wanted me in the Angel healing room, sitting at the person's feet, keeping my hands up to stabilize and enhance the field. In each session a pure angelic frequency was transmitted. The Angels showed her things. She said it was like a big television screen inside her head. She just described what she saw. In each session, the Guardian Angels and the Angels of healing came, bringing the most appropriate light frequencies for that person.

As my perception refined, I could experience more of their subtle work. What at first seemed like whorls of light had different qualities of color, strength, clarity, and brilliance. Our spirit doctor, Dr. Kirk, came in to assist. He focused fine beams of colored light precisely within that strong field. Often he did procedures or used techniques that were later accepted by the medical establishment.

The healing was complete on the level of the etheric or light body at the end of the session. If the person could allow it to precipitate down into the physical, then it would hold. Playing Dorie's healing tape softly each night helped recreate the session and the healing.

When she spoke the words, describing what Dr. Kirk and the Angels were doing, I saw exactly what she was describing. My own sight developed; what was latent and dormant became active in this strong field. As we continued working together, there came a time when, if she got tired, she could pass the small microphone to me in the middle of a session. We were seeing the same pictures, the energy field was so strong and steady, either of us could say the words.

Angel Healing Circles

When Dorie was working with the Angels, holding public and private sessions, it was in another time and way of living. She lived in Carmel-by-the-Sea, an artistic and creative colony on the central coast of California. Women still walked to the post office in their housedresses. The mail was not delivered because addresses were too imprecise, so mornings at the post office were the Meet-up of the day.

She was one of the "grande dames" of Carmel's spiritual community, which included New Thought, Unity, Presbyterian, Catholic, Christian Science, Methodist, and Episcopalian. She was known and respected for her inherent wisdom, kindness, and deep humility.

Her healing circles grew from a few people saying prayers for others to more than eighty people most weeks. Shopkeeper closed their shops to come. These were simple, joy-filled, inspired gatherings. The results were real. People felt soothed. They experienced healings. Situations suddenly reversed. Miracles, small and large, became the way life could be.

Each week people told Angel stories, things that happened in sudden or seemingly impossible ways. We all became comfortable saying the words of the healing prayers. One person sat in the center of the circle. Dorie looked around and asked someone to say the words. That person then stood in the center with hands on the shoulders of the seated one. Starting, "Dear Angels . . ." and the words began. No one knew ahead of time what to say. No one refused. Each time the prayer was beautiful, profound, perfect for the person seated, and also marvelously perfect for the inner healing of the one who said the words. Each time it was this way. Each week, week after week, for all the years she held the healing circles.

She was the only person talking about the Angels at that time. She was not affiliated with any large religious organization; rather, she started her own church—The Church of Self Discovery—because self-discovery was her lifelong interest and passion. She studied various forms of meditation, exercise, good nutrition, alternative therapies, and the new ways of moving energy that were being investigated at that time. She was always reading stories of inspiration and news of medical breakthroughs that often corroborated the light techniques our spirit doctor used in the healing sessions.

Working with her I saw miracles: bones mended, burns healed over night, tumors diminished and dissolved. Fear, worry, and mental anguish were "spells" that she and the Angels broke. Hope and gratitude were the take-away gifts we received from each gathering.

Forces of Light

There was no question of not believing when I was with Dorie. But sometimes when I was alone, doubts could come. What was I doing here? Why was it me who was here? Why was I the one who stayed when the other girls had to go—you know, got married, got pulled away by family responsibilities or financial obligations? No one was pulling me, and nothing in the world was more compelling than being there. Where were my doubts coming from?

One afternoon I went to walk on a hidden curve of land near the mouth of the Carmel River. I lay out on the smooth sand to ask and to pray. "Thank you, my dear Angels, for being with me today. I want only to know you, to feel you with me here, just as I am. Please take away my doubt and let me know. May I see your shining face." I felt like a small child, so suddenly earnest and clear. My voice was cracking. This was not my mind; it was my heart praying.

My body seemed to slip deeper into the sand or I dissolved out of it. There was a great sparkling on the water. It moved over me and whirled around me. It felt like tiny kisses of light. They formed into streams, finer than wisps, glittering minutely and twirling. I felt my whole self hollow out. Spots or clumps of stodgy energy showed on the inner curves of my cranium and inside my body cavity. I can't tell how I knew, but I felt the sticky consistency of them as thought patterns that held self-doubt. I prayed to be free of these old patterns, "Please, my Angels, help me to be one with your light."

When I said yes to the force of light, those murky places started to disperse. They were caught up into the swirling. I could only let this soft blessing into all my being. I was the entire cosmos and the swirling nebulae. With my head against the sand, I heard, "You were made of the same stuff as the stars."

I was this big open thing strung with cords of light. The wind moved through me as waves of bliss. Then all was calm. Tiny ripples moved across the water.

"O blessed Angels, thank you for your love. Let me live in the truth that you have shown me. Let this grace flow through me. Let me share your graceful presence."

In the Angel Room

In California, you have to be either a beautician, a reverend, or a massage therapist in order to touch people, to lay on hands. If I was going to work with Dorie, I would need to be one of those. At that time in my life, massage therapy looked like the best choice, and I had some natural healing skills. So for my birthday Dorie gave me tuition for massage school.

The classes were held in a large mirrored room that functioned primarily as a dance studio. Our massage tables were stored on giant hooks around the room and taken down as we needed them. On one particular evening about halfway through the course, we students had just started to gather in a small circle in the center of this enormous room. We'd just had our first anatomy class in the lab of a local community college. Having seen our first cadaver, we were discussing the feelings that brought up. Twenty of us in a small circle talking.

Without warning and with no visible means, one massage table unhooked itself from the wall. It sailed across the entire room and struck me on the head. I was knocked out but retained inner awareness. The instructor gathered me up and carried me to his car to bring me to the hospital, thirty minutes away. I do not remember that drive or the time in the emergency room, where some tests were performed. It was decided that I had a slight concussion. I could go home but someone had to stay with me, watch me, and wake me up every few hours to make sure I knew my name and where I was. But where to take me?

The instructor and all the class members knew Dorie and had great love for her. So they just drove to her house at ten o'clock at night. Dorie's husband, Andre, never let anyone stay there because he had such trouble sleeping. But this time Dorie said, "Of course. Put her in the Angel room." My classmates all wanted to stay in that room with me, but one fellow was chosen to be my waker-upper.

I felt fine in the morning, but when I looked in the mirror I could see my eyes were all kitty-wampus. This went on for many days. Dorie and I walked slowly around the block in the afternoons, holding hands as we always did. She confided, "Now you know how I feel." She said, "The Angels have done this to keep you near to me. Andre would not have let you in, but I need you now."

She told me she'd had a few knocks on the head in her life, and they were big leaps in consciousness. It had happened to her and now it happened to me. And so I began living in the Angel room.

Dorie's Passing

I lived and studied with Dorie only a few precious years. I met her in October 1981. On my birthday in September of 1983, we decided it was the time to formalize our kinship. We had talked about the possibilities, but on that day we made it official. In keeping with the great spiritual traditions where the deep truths are carried on in alternating generations, Dorie adopted me as granddaughter/next of kin. I could have almost been her daughter, but granddaughter just felt right.

She named me and I took the name D'Angelo as my profound honor, to use henceforward on all things. We lit candles and thanked the Angels for bringing us together and for their continued blessing. Someone else officiated as we spoke. Dorie held her hands over my heart. In the middle of a pool of sunlight, on a day unlike any other, she passed to me her wisdom, like sliding goodness from a silver platter into my heart.

On that day she also certified that I had completed a course in the practice of God's healing through the grace of the healing Angels and the Guardian Angels. That certificate was the first time we used my new name. It was done.

Lyman, Dorie's cousin from Canada, was visiting at the time. He had a new kind of wristwatch that could flash words under the face. (This was 1983. There were no computers or iPhones.) Since he was teaching us how to use his invention, the Percussor, he had the watch keyed to show a slogan about it.

At the diner table that night, we toasted my new name. Andre was in complete agreement and welcomed me into the family. Lyman changed his watch face to flash, "Jenny D'Angelo Heals Pain." We all laughed together.

I was well-trained and steady in my sight. I could do the Angel sessions and say the words of healing. I was utterly devoted to Dorie. We were ready to go out and tell the world about the Angels. Then just before Thanksgiving, Dorie had an embolism, a blood clot in her leg. The doctors got it easily. But the few days in the hospital had an impact. When she was home again, Dorie told me she was ready now and wanted to live with the Angels full-time.

She was supposed to be a guest speaker at the conference of wellness and faith held annually at the near-by Asilomar Conference Center. The main speaker, Dr. Paul Brenner, instead came to see her. He had been teaching a method of silent communication, wherein his body gave him signals that he learned to hear as yes and no. He was coming to support Dorie and fine tune her inner knowing at this crucial moment. I remember it so well.

Paul arrived. Dorie said, "I want only Jenny." So I sat in a chair in alert stillness as she and Paul worked. She held a question in her mind. Paul felt in his body the response. At the end of their session, Dorie was entirely at peace in herself. She asked Paul to please assist her by telling the family.

He went out to the living room to tell Andre what had transpired. Andre, a small man, was so angry that he picked up Paul, a man over six feet tall, and bodily threw him out the front door.

[When I later saw Paul, he looked deeply at me, shook his head, and simply said, "To be a woman and a healer—it's tough. It's not going to be easy."]

Dorie asked me to move my mattress into her room, to be by the foot of her bed. She took off her wedding rings and gave them to me, saying, "You have my hands; you should have my rings." She stopped taking food and water. She was not in pain. We played music that she loved. We read passages aloud. Mostly I held her hands. She died peacefully and in full consciousness in my arms three days later.

Then she gave me her greatest gift. She let me go with her for an instant. As I held her, I saw the Angels take her soul from out of her body, out of the top of her head. I saw it so clearly. In that splendid, stunning, and blazing instant, they let me go with her. There is a "there," although it is surely not a place, but it is a placement of magnificent light. I knew that absolutely and certainly. This certainty gave me comfort. It gives me comfort still. I am not afraid. I am only grateful that we had the time of our lives together.

Soon after she passed the phone started ringing. People from all over the world, people who knew Dorie and had had sessions with her, called to say she had just appeared in their room. From Sydney, New York, Los Angeles, London, Toronto, she was giving blessings to all. I felt her very close. In that week I was not sad; I was filled with a deep calming peace and a great love. Some call it the healing rapture.

At week's end we held her Celebration of Life at the Boy Scouts Hall, following her wishes. More than 350 people attended, told Angel stories from the past or of her recent visits. We stood in circle. On that most honorable day, in full view and with the blessing of the Angels, Andre placed his hands on my shoulders and said, "Now I place the mantle on you." The room was full of splendid light. No eye was dry. Joy and loss and wonder mixed.

The Politics of Death

There is politics after death. I didn't know it, but it operated strongly in 1984. When wise and radiant Dorie passed, the circle around her went into disarray. She had wanted me to continue, but after a few weeks, it was clear I could not. Andre suddenly appeared at the Angel Circle and kicked me out in a rage. His energy roared out in a thunderous red wave with a violent punch. It absolutely thrust me out. People were divided. I was too young and I was not Dorie.

We used to say that Andre carried the darkness so that Dorie could carry all the light. Maybe that was the soul agreement they had. Maybe that was necessary in order for her to be the Angel Lady, but now that arrangement was over and I had to get out fast. He began a lawsuit against me, claiming he alone knew what Dorie was about, that what he called the "Angel power" was his.

I kept my trust with Dorie and continued to offer Angel sessions, but I felt unready to fight Andre. I moved to a small apartment with a friend and quietly grew my practice of healing and massage. The Angels were always brilliant and shining in the sessions, but I avoided public gatherings, did not advertise, and gave up the larger dream I had shared with Dorie, to tell all the world about the Angels.

My training as an editor led to regular freelance work. I worked for most of the publishers on the West Coast, often editing or proofing spiritual texts. A good balance then, of body work, healing, and editing. Again I began to build a new life.

* * * * *

Looking at it now, I would say Andrew Harvey came into my life as much more than the higher octave of Andre. By his vision and his unwavering support, we are breaking the old black spell cast so long ago.

The Gracious Light

Writing these pages full of memory and love has been a deepening experience for me. I had lived the changes but not fully acknowledged the direct "hand" of the Angels at nearly every turn. Car accidents, mysterious flying massage tables, and a spirit doctor operating from higher realms were the outer manifestations of the inner trust that was building. It was not a straight road by any means, but it was a direct path.

My love for Dorie and trust in her were unwavering. In her energetic field I had no doubts. But I saw how it was with some people. They came, maybe the husband coming along with his wife because she had the cancer, but he drove her and wanted her to be better, whatever it took—even seeing a faith healer. Maybe Dorie was already talking with the woman and I was sitting with the man. He would be nervous and shy. He might just whisper to me, "Do you really believe this stuff?" No one would ever say that to Dorie. She lived in trust and service. The steadiness of her belief helped people to believe in her and the Angels. At least the possibility of Angels. And the possibility of healing.

Coming to see Dorie usually meant a person was desperate. All the regular ways to proceed had been exhausted; now there were only radical options. So to walk in to her sweet living room and have her hold your hands already started the releasing.

I saw how the healings worked. Once you let the Angels into your field they could begin. The pure light was directed into each of the specific places that held the old blacknesses, the old thought patterns, the pain. At the moment of the healing, all there was, was light. The person was filled with peace and with clear, pure light. That light held hope. If the person could allow it, every kind of healing was possible.

Dorie believed that everyone had within themselves the perfect pattern of their perfect self. This blueprint of perfect functioning could be activated. The cells could remember. Simple words carried clear truth. Dorie's deep belief was grounded in her own experience. This gave the person a ground for believing too. If the person could open to the healing as it was happening and accept the healing as complete when the session was over, he or she could carry it forward out into life. I saw miraculous things happen in this way.

The Angels were so gracious. They were doing the same leading by light with me that they did in the healing sessions. There was no place to be but where I was, doing precisely what I was doing. I could answer anyone, "Yes, I do believe."

I forgave myself for my naïve and irrational behaviors; they all had led me to Dorie. Her love was steady as the Earth. I could let my love blossom.

I stayed with Dorie because living in this field with her and the Angels was healing all of me. I gave my time and my devotion in exchange for having a seat at the home of unconditional love.

Bewildering

By 1988 I had begun to drive to Santa Cruz to hear a charismatic Unity minister, Emily Sanford. I became a regular commuter/attendee because of the vibrant shot-in-the-arm she and this congregation gave me. On the Sunday celebrating the birth of Rev. Martin Luther King, Jr., the theme of having a dream was naturally highlighted. In the silence of the guided meditation at the heart of the service, the Angels spoke quite clearly and distinctly to me, "We are moving to Santa Cruz. Are you coming?"

My deep connection to the Monterey Peninsula was related to Dorie. She had passed. Andre was raging against me. I was ready to start a new life again. I moved four months later.

The Angels still appeared in every healing session, as did my spirit doctor, Dr. Kirk. After a time, Dorie began to be part of the healing sessions as well. The energy she brought was the same pure love that I knew when she was incarnate. Intense, penetrating blue, her beautiful blue. Often she worked on the hearts of the people on my table. Her love was tangible and her beautiful hands were in front of my eyes.

I say again that I have never known the Angels to fail. In every single session they came with their shining lovelight. So I was carrying in my heart a pure, clean vibration.

But the world was changing. People were beginning to take note of the Angels in a very particular way. Figures of Angels were appearing on the covers of magazines. They filled the windows of fancy shops and not just at Christmas. They peered over the pages of catalogues. There were whole stores selling Angel figurines, jewelry, statuary, and clothing. Angels were used to sell every manner of thing. Even Victoria's Secret had Angels.

There were conferences. There were seminars. There were workshops and expos. I could have gone to these workshops; I could have led them. Imagine a whole room of people talking about Angels, believing in Angels. This was just what Dorie had wanted, to help all the people know about Angels, to have a relation with the Angels. This was supposed to be the shining and welcoming entry into a way of being in the world, living with the Angels.

I should have been happy, I kept on telling myself. But my heart turned away from all the hoopla. It felt like a circus. The more the magazines published stories about Angels, the more the conferences had advertisements for Angel portraits and Angel wear, the more confused I felt. Seeing Angels in all the shop windows saddened me, because it did not open anyone to the incredible love and guidance of the Angels.

I knew from Dorie that to have a relation with the Angels was a natural but profound blessing. They were God's personal gift to us and we could only receive them in awe and humility. She might not say the word, but she lived every day a humble and surrendered life.

My great good fortune had been to learn from someone so pure. Dorie was a humble, ordinary woman who happened to be completely illuminated. She lived in a very simple way, yet she offered the purest transmission of the truth of the Angels. I learned from her and experienced directly their grace and power. Quietly, but in continual amazement—that is the mystery of surrender.

In My Home Town

I was still a daughter and on occasion made visit to my mother back in Massachusetts. I was not married, had no children; my life made no sense to her. She was quite loud in her manner and could be extremely rude in public. It was hard to be together, but I tried, by having short visits.

My mother really wanted me to take her to Temple one Friday night. She just wanted me to be normal and sit with her. I was glad to take her, but in my heart, I could not go inside. I couldn't force myself. I said I'd drive her and wait for her. I would be her private chauffeur.

Living in the same four rooms with her was difficult. News or talk shows on the radio or the TV, very loud, day and night. She wanted constant chatter and agreement to her negativity, nagging on about people and events. I was desperate for some silence, looking forward to some few minutes alone. I wanted to frame the twilight by myself, meditate in the car in my old home town.

After the service, she came tromping out to the car. She stood at my door, one hand foisting her purse in the air, the other hand wagging at me. There were big furrows on her forehead.
"How did you do it?" she accused me. Her voice was having a temper tantrum.
"How did you do it? The whole sermon was about Angels.
I didn't even know *we* had Angels."

I didn't say a word.

* * * * *

In the 90s I was back in my home town, a decade after the time with Dorie. My sister and I were packing up my mother's apartment to move her to an assisted-living facility. It was the last time I would be in that town.

I knew I had to go to my father's grave. He had died thirty years before. It had been traumatic for me, not only because he was my dad and I loved him. But he died suddenly, just three days before I was to leave for England and my time at Oxford University. My big leap of freedom was encircled in a long loop of tears because of his sudden death.

This would be my opportunity to revisit the cemetery. I could place a small angel stone on his headstone, mixing the Jewish tradition with the Angel ways.

The old Jewish cemetery was still kept by the same family. They had index cards with family names and plot designations. The man showed me the way, but let off leading me when we got "in the neighborhood." I recognized names from the community of my childhood. Then my uncle Hans. Then my father's stone.

It was a shock to see the name of my father chiseled in a slab of granite. And his dates. The last one, the one I remember keenly. So shattering to my youthful dreams. I stood before it. Bits of dirty slush still on the ground. It would have to be like that—the weather in that town was singularly cold and fraught with blizzards late in the spring.

I didn't say a formal prayer. I simply quieted myself, dropped my attention down into my heart. I wanted to be with his spirit in a very simple way. The site and the name on the stone helped to stir and then quiet my emotions.

I hadn't known my father very well. That was not the way with men from Germany of the last century. And my mother managed all the fire power in the family. He was pushed more and more to the side and then the back. He died suddenly at age 68, an old man.

So I stood at his stone and loved him. The air rippled before me like a velvet river.

Then a clear voice sounded in my head. It ran down my left side, circled my heart, washed down the length of my body. I was not frightened in the least. I was utterly clear and present in that expanded moment.

The Voice said, *This is where the good and the kind come from. This is the good and the kind.*

Across time he came to bless me. I thanked the Angels for being with him wherever he was. I felt entirely at peace with him, the good man who had been my father.

Shaking and Connecting

Santa Cruz was unusual, eccentric, creative, and funky in many ways, so it afforded me a kind of normalcy within its fresh environment. I was invited to hold Angel Healing Circles at Unity Temple. I was able to find work writing and editing, and I could still offer healing and body work sessions on the week-ends.

Then in October 1989 there was the Loma Prieta earthquake. No one there will forget those five minutes of 7.2 magnitude, and then those hundreds of aftershocks, night after night. It was humbling. My apartment was not badly damaged, just a waist-high pile of broken dishes and glass fragments, spices, teas, and grains in the middle of the kitchen.

As the world shook, I had to go back to my core . . . again. I looked to my inner world for a sense of stability. The earthquake demonstrated that it was not in the outer world, even if I had survived. In January 1990, I began working for a small and dynamic publishing company in the redwoods. We published thoughtful and excellent spiritual titles for the general public.

One week-end I was invited to attend a Light Body workshop put on by one of our authors. In the closing circle on Sunday morning I was filled with a marvelous energy and light. One participant in the circle ran up to me afterwards and said, "I could see you from across the room. Whatever you have, I want."

That was Gisela, a wild and smart Swiss doctor who had recently moved here. She and her husband had keen interest in Light Body work. She was seeing the light I knew. Different vocabularies, but the same light.

We began to study and work together. My years of meditation paralleled her years as a doctor of psychiatry; my years of massage and her years of process work. We had a strong synergy that supported both of our minds and our souls. We decided to put our work together and teach seminars.

In a striking blue pyramid building in Zurich we introduced these two kinds of subtle seeing and sensing–Angels and Light Body. The precision of the Light Body work resonated in the Swiss mind of clarity; it softened and opened everyone so that the Angels could just flood in. Then the pure vibration could be integrated in a deep way. It was a good experience to bring to that environment.

We sensed that very old patterns of thought in the air, in the culture, in the mountains of Switzerland were starting to unravel. For me, this also included patterns from my time in the ashram. The good-old Swiss ways could not continue—at least that's how it felt when we invoked the light and the Angels. Our current friendship was intermingled with old family stories from the war. We felt our own inner work had threads to the past and that the healing work we did together was helping our families and our ancestors heal as well.

We worked and studied together for a few years. Then other threads took over prominence in both our lives and our ways diverged.

Training/refined perception

I have been training all my life in the methods of refined perception. From the start I was a miracle baby, born three months premature and weighing only two-and-one-half pounds, I lived for those three months in an incubator, hovering between life and death.

I was able to go back to the incubator a few times, to that first moment of breath, the nurse who held me, tiny as a game hen, in her palm. She looked at me and said, "Poor thing. She can't hope to live." When she placed me in the glass box, the doctor said casually, "And if she does live, she'll surely have brain damage."

I believe that premature birth, three months not in the womb, has metaphorically allowed me this thin skin, so sensitive that I am able to see light. I believe it also started a seed of isolation, to be alone for long periods, comfortable in my skin, and in my self.

Meditation in the ashram in Switzerland, high above the level of thought forms, supported a more refined nervous system. This allowed for the most subtle of perceptions and the growth of innate knowing.

When I met Dorie, after the silence of the ashram, the heart's need for love was answered. She adopted me as granddaughter/next of kin, blessed in the sight of the Angels. The field of lovelight was a tangible force field. Dorie passed directly into my heart the pure love of the Angels and their unwavering, unconditional care. I was licensed in massage therapy and could practice hands-on healing.

I subsequently studied various meditation practices and had the privilege of sitting with the Dalai Lama, Ammachi, Gurumayi, and American-born teacher, Gangaji, in the lineage of Ramana Maharshi. The essential heart practice of self-inquiry was a diamond turning in me. I had clear and deep experiences whenever I sat in the company of these saints and teachers.

I continued working with the Angels, sometimes bringing them into the silence at the end of a bodywork session. I studied many methods of healing directly from their creators. Modalities included Zero Balancing, Rosen Method bodywork, New Decision Therapy, Process Acupressure. In the desert of Arizona, I stood in circle with the remarkable Drunvalo Melchizedek, participating in the healing for Earth and Sky.

Integrating these modalities in my work, I maintained a successful healing practice on the central coast for more than thirty years.

Training/words & poetry

Drawn to words and poetry I began writing at an early age. In high school I entered a poetry contest and met poet Archibald MacLeish, with whom I had a long correspondence—my first igniting. I completed a degree in English at U. Mass, during which time I met Robert Bly at the first "Poets Against the War" reading in 1968. I continued my education at Oxford University, then lived in London selling rare books at a distinguished old book shop.

I worked as a free-lance editor for many independent publishers in northern California, including Houghton-Mifflin, Hampton-Brown, Crossing Press, and Aslan Publishers, as well as editing manuscripts for individual authors.

Hired as a part-time editor, I soon became the full-time Personal Assistant to Robert Dilts, a highly-respected author and international trainer in the world of NLP. Neuro-Linguistic Programming originated in Santa Cruz, where NLP University was held every summer. Robert traveled extensively, yet called in each day from wherever he was in the world. I managed all aspects of his office with responsibilities that were intricate and wide-ranging. It was a solitary position, but I was used to working alone, and it gave me a huge amount of freedom. Through NLPU I had contact with world-class trainers, many of whom became personal friends. In all, it was an excellent environment in which to integrate the strands of my life in a deep and elegant way.

Robert began using my poems in his seminars. My love of poetry and training as a healer came together when we produced an audio CD entitled *Light from the Tip of the Tongue*. Offered through Journey to Genius Productions, it presented a personal poetic journey framed in light. The poems wove an experiential field, established a resonance. When a listener heard the words, a light field was created and emotions could surface. Healings could happen.

Dorie taught me about the magnetics of recording. The voice has a great capacity to transmit consciousness. In her time, the radio waves amplified the power. She did many healings over the radio and the effects were real. In a more modern format, that power was quantified. I saw the CD as a sequel to the Angel healing tapes we made in the 80s. It was my offering to the great healing power of the universe.

Build-up

It was an excellent time for me, satisfying and rewarding. Working for nearly a decade in the same position, I was able to buy a small house in Santa Cruz. I hung it with prayer flags, smudged all the rooms. In the back, where the four neighboring property lines met, stood a huge old cypress, a heritage tree. I blessed this elder of the neighborhood, saying, "Let us live together well, in safety and beauty."

I asked the Angels to enter and live with me. "Let there be peacefulness and contentment. Let there be love within these walls. Let there be healings. My dear Angels, let the walls be filled up with blessed and happy times."

A tiny front yard wild with Shasta daisies and iris, untamed by the weathered fence; a back yard overhung with wisteria and jasmine, deep red roses poking through masses of alstroemeria. A corner to sit in the slanting chairs and watch the shore birds that flew through on their annual migration. One thousand steps from the Pacific, my little bungalow, home at last.

To actually put down roots was a massive shift in focus. I now owned property and I was committed to staying. I began to keep chickens that laid green eggs. I started to swim laps in a public pool five minutes away. I made some investments. I wrote and read in more poetry events and was invited to join a long-running critique group, the Emerald Street Poets. There I met skilled and wonderful poets, including the remarkable and beloved Kathleen. Finally another kindred soul with whom I could talk of God and poetry and Angels and beauty. We could plunge the depths, not afraid to dream. Life was good.

Loss

Within a few years my life was in another whirlwind. My excellent boss changed his life dramatically and moved his base of operation to Paris. It was an agonizing process but when it was done, I had no job, no health insurance, no unemployment benefits. The economic recession started just then and I was part of it. My investments were lost in a Madoff-like scandal. Almost everything I had built up was gone and I was hanging on to my house by a thread.

In a very short time my beautiful friend Kathleen, valiant fighter and holder of such gracious light, died. The Angels organized that I be there, for she had rallied, and she wanted me to be with her for Easter sunrise. But, instead, on that holy morn, I saw her leave her limbs, gradually and without pain. Drastic remnant of a glorious being, we washed and dressed her in roses and gold, perfumed those stark bones with fragrant oils.

Waiting at the mortuary the next day, Kathleen spoke to me just below my normal hearing, *Don't be sad for me. Don't be sad for you either. You knew the love. You know the love. You are the love. This is the truth of who you are. I am happy when you are. Please don't be sad.*

In a wash of grief and awe I helped create a memorial service for her. Tears streamed down my face while she, radiant Kathleen, talked to me in clear, bright, shining tones. The simple words, *Don't be sad. Don't be sad.* She was singing the *Don't Be Sad Rag.* All the many days after her passing, she talked with me on nearly every one.

The next month, the good husband of one of my oldest friends suddenly died in the night. She called me in her distress. Three weeks later she too, suddenly gone. I could secure some comfort in sensing they were together, but it was shaky ground. When in the next month another person, and then another, and then another passed—six friends in six months—I was done. I was just arms and legs and heartache. A shard in the sand, vessel broken open, bits cast about.

I was desperate and wretched but I was not afraid. Everything was already stripped away. No avoidance. No distraction. It was just me and God. The series of catastrophes forced me to face death and every dark corner in my self and my world of belief. I joined a hospice grief group; I was not dealing with the loss of a spouse or a parent as most were, but this cumulative and wide-ranging loss had hollowed out my self and washed me away.

I just kept myself and my chickens. I walked to the ocean. I swam laps. I got a bag of groceries from the senior outreach, got culls from the markets for the chickens and me. I lost all shame and was grateful for this use of resources. There was always enough to eat.

My training was to pay attention, to write, to meditate, and to pray. Kathleen talked to me all the time. I was grateful for her grace, even if I could not always take her comfort. In that period, my entire life seemed sorrow-laden, triggered and now connected to her delicate passing. Most of my closest friends, ones who knew Dorie too, many younger than me, were gone. It wasn't so much depression as a naked and stark questioning.

All I could do was step into the darkness, step into the silence. Stay as present as possible to the fluctuations of feelings and emotions as they came up. I lived slowly, made no plans. Waves of sadness rolled in with revelations. Intimacy with those across the veil was keener and clearer than with any people alive. I breathed with the women of my lineage, sisters of my father. Inner cleansing and release burst through me and rippled back across time.

After a night of sickness, chills, and fever, I wrote in my journal:

> Kind of rather glorious: The very pain that hurts the most, is the oldest, reminds us back, terribly and swiftly. If we go, again and again to that dark trough, the spirit horses will eventually come and drink, and the story will be completed.
>
> Way down in those recesses, old tears, old habits re-creating the same drama again. Inside the swirl, it is so real. How could you possibly not feel it? It is calling to you to feel it, say it, cry it. Feel it. And release.

In so vulnerable a state, simple living was all I could do. It was just one moment at a time. It took everything I had. And slowly it strengthened me. In facing enormous sadness I was given the grace of seeing bonds break into illuminating freedom.

A delicate place. It was familiar, being between dimensions. The Angels had shown me in countless ways that they were the silver doorway between the dimensions. Now they were my comforters, gentle guardians of my shattered heart.

* * * *

I applied for and got a scholarship to attend the Conference of the Great Mother and the New Father, a grand conclave that Robert Bly and other poets, artists, thinkers, storytellers, and musicians had convened annually since 1975. His work and his workshops had always deeply inspired and stirred me. If I was to find a reason to continue, it would be in the company of the old master, whom I adored, and these wild creators.

I arrived at the rustic camp, on the shores of Lake Damariscotta in Maine. Over the long lake, the loons called out mournfully. A perfect welcome to me, who had been crying the whole way there. On the first night, the ferocious kindness of Robert Bly poured into me as we heard his poem, written freshly for us.

Keeping Our Small Boat Afloat

So many blessings have been given us
During the first distribution of light, that we are
Admired in a thousand galaxies for our grief.

Don't expect us to appreciate creation or to
Avoid mistakes. Each of us is a latecomer
To the earth, picking up wood for the fire.

~ ~ ~ ~ ~

It's hard to grasp how much generosity
Is involved in letting us go on breathing,
When we contribute nothing valuable but our grief.

Each of us deserves to be forgiven, if only for
Our persistence in keeping our small boat afloat
When so many have gone down in the storm.

With grief as our contribution, these words broke over me. My tears came then in humility and gratitude that there could be a reason, this small boat. My heart was pierced by the goodness and creativity of this tribe, of whom I could be a part. Old as trees. Old as blood. Old as sound.

I woke at dawn in surprising quietness of mind and began each day with singing in circle. Brilliant poets and storytellers stirred our collective minds and hearts. I learned the no-mind of drumming under the clear stars as fires burned hot in our faces. There were lively and soulful conversations over delicious camp food. I canoed around the islands, saw the loons up close. Jumped off the wooden dock yelling like a schoolgirl, swam in the snow melt water, watched patterns of pollen turn to sprinkled gold on the lake edge. When the week was over, I was renewed in spirit, inspired of heart, and refreshed in body.

A dove grey dawn. Kathleen's dawn. Her day, her Easter. One year later.

The morning she slipped away and nearly every day since, she had been talking and laughing and cajoling my flickering self, shocking me out and back to some kind of knowing. Always the silver slip of light that connected me to her and thus to all. On that last day of the mourning year, she spoke clearly and boldly, the same words, "Don't be sad."

> Oh Jenny, it is glorious here. All the best of every thing and no entanglements. Everyone clearly only love and truth. What we shared, those many high, clear moments, that's what it's like here, for everyone, all the time. We glimpsed it. We knew it. Now I know it. I send you everyday—love, love, love—just like before, only more and no suffering. Please don't suffer for me. I am one with all there is. I love you forever, just like always.

Sorrow is for growing deeper. It is for knowing more. All the people of the world know sorrow, but in each woman's heart, in each man's heart, sorrow lays a different seed thought—that old hard nugget. This extravagance of wings when sorrow takes flight. This deep tendril to the soul of the earth, stretching down to the bottom of grief.

I must have absolutely chosen to know so many kinds of sorrow, loss, and loneliness, and come out alive again, so that a deeper, wider vision could be given to me. From the bottom of the well of sorrow I had crawled out. Up from deep earth, remembering through my fingers, the brown earth, tree bark splinters, driftwood boughs, finally to breathe cool air. Happiness tempered by sadness, like the silky, translucent skin of a soap bubble, shimmering for a minute in the afternoon light.

* * * *

The Angels have said so many times, *You have never been forsaken. You have never been abandoned.*

Back Again with More

After more than a decade my friendship with Gisela resurfaced in 2008. She called me, truly out of the blue. She said she suddenly knew she had to be back in contact with me. She had been bitten by a rattlesnake on her land and nearly died. She was even more sensitive and could only be with people and things that resonated with her and touched her soul.

It was also my darkest time. I felt I was only a remnant of the self she knew. I had lost so much on so many levels. I was not sure how I could survive.

We both hungered for the talks we used to have, talks of light and Angels and the nature of the universe. As we gently picked up the rhythm of conversation, we saw ourselves and the light get stronger. It was something like a corridor connecting both locations, she on her mountain miles away, me in my cottage in the fog by the sea.

One day Gisela said, "Hey, I can help you. Let me help you. You are so valuable to me. You introduced me to the living Angels. They are now in my energy field and part of the energy of my land. I am so grateful. I get so much support from you. It is my joy to help you. Let me help you."

She said her family had always helped people in their village in Switzerland and now it could be me whom she helped. Not a big deal. From her heart of kindness, she quietly became my benefactor. Each month she helped me cover my bills. Each month I was blessed to continue living in my home.

The mysterious hand of grace had touched me again. The idea that someone would think enough of me to want to help me so graciously and generously was absolutely stunning. An astounding set of circumstances had brought me to such a state of humility and now to grace. I could only be open. It was not me making such elegant arrangements out of my crumpled days.

I had to be attentive to my thoughts. I could not say, "There is no one to help me." I had to catch myself every time an old thought like that came up. It was not true. I could not think ill of my circumstances; I could only bless my good fortune.

Gisela helped me through the hardest time. When her support ended, I could only see the whole experience of loss and saving grace as an expression of the hand of the Angels and the Divine Mother.

Work Made Visible

One of the blessings from the life and passing of Kathleen was my association with WomenCare, a unique support center for women with and surviving cancer. She was leading writing groups there and suddenly asked me if I could take over her slot the next day. They said it would be OK, even if I wasn't a cancer survivor. Just this once I could help out. Kathleen thought I would love it and I did, immediately.

I brought in luminous poems and read them slowly out loud. I told the women to just let any words or phrases connect with them in any way, be it memory or wish or dream. Anything, riff out on anything, just touch pen to paper and let go.

We came together to unburden and explore and create. Each session we held each other in our hearts. Something more than writing happened. The Angels overlit the whole group and the light became palpable in the room. How much brighter and easier things seemed when we were together, laughing and crying, feeling raw, alive, and true. Some ease allowed the body's natural healing power. Some experience of grace . . . and two hours out of pain. The women were free of pain in the time that we were together.

And so I was fortunate to lead groups there for five years. Some of the best hours were with these women. There was no falseness. It was truth and heart and flashing insight and genuine imagination that made those sessions so rich and healing.

After one session, the Angels wrote of the group:

> You think those tears are fresh and only yours, but they are tears from all the ancestors, all their longing and their pain too. When you let your precious tears tip out of your eyes, it is freeing them as well as yourself. A simple and tender joy, this, to let the tears come. Let them be the path of connection to past and to future. A path to communion and community of spirit. Your healing can contribute to the greater good. One word and one tear can stream you straight into gladness.

I bowed to the commingling of wonder and surprise. I blessed whatever it was made us open so willingly. I honored the sacred listening. It was the work of the heart to listen awake inside. That was all I knew and it's what we did together. It was a privilege to be there.

Bless

Don't dawdle on this path today.
Don't you feel the light pouring down?
Don't you feel those twinkling particles of stellar light
entering your perfect cells?

Our star family that is all of love infills us now
as we prepare for the coming season on the New Earth.
I know it is true and feel the subtle resonance with light
as we sit here together.

There is a specter of illness, but in this room today
we find love. We express the love that lives in us.
We find ourselves connected by the vigorous
truth revealed in open-hearted sharing.

We proclaim our strength and steadfastness
by coming here. And when we leave this
safe chamber of truth-telling, we will be
walking in our solid and steady feet of love.

WomenCare
11 December 2011

How Does It Really Work, This Living with the Angels?

1.

On the exact day, eleven years after Dorie passed, I was spending the afternoon with Sally. She had known Dorie before I was even on the scene, and hers had been one of the homes I lived in when I was working with Dorie. She has since passed also, but on that day in 1995, we remembered together.

Right at the time Dorie breathed her last breaths, we felt a stabbing sadness. Between noon and 1:00 PM Sally and I were swiftly and suddenly thrust into a deep episode of grief and anguish at Dorie's quick passing. We cried together, surprised at the intensity of memory and longing. As if those days had been all idyll, tranquil bliss.

Then the Angels offered me—in a way I could not refuse—the possibility of an energetic clearing. I was given an utterly clear experience of remembering, brought back directly to the moments of Dorie's passing. I was on her bed with her, holding her in my arms. Andre had turned her head and whispered into her ear not too softly, "You are mine. You will always be mine. We will be together throughout time."

On that day, eleven years later, I could understand his anger and his jealousy, which could not be directly expressed. And in the long moment that it took me to feel it all again, I could forgive him his fury and resentment. I could forgive his clinging on to her. I could forgive him his rage.

In my body, it felt the same way as when Dr. Kirk cut a person's chords to this realm. My solar plexus felt hugely free to open, an aperture of grace now. It felt for me like a great clearing of Andre.

Then, immediately, the sense, vivid and tangible, of Dorie being inside of me completely. Not Dorie the dear person, but Dorie the name for the frequency, what we call the Presence of Angels. I saw how they were completely inside and through me, how they also streamed at my hands and feet. The Angelic Presence was always in me. My job was to be present to it.

2.

I am writing this page the day after my friend Bruce passed. We were with him, 12 or 13 people in his room in the rehab center. The head nurse had called and we knew this was his day. One of his oldest friends touched his hand softly, straightened the pillows that cushioned his arms. She spread the red fuzzy blanket around his limbs and the pillows. She stroked his face so tenderly, softly murmuring, "We're here with you. We got you."

His many musician friends began to sing his favorite boogie tunes. Someone knew he wanted "When the Saints" so one man played it gently on the mandolin. We sang "Swing Low" in the individual keys of our trembling voices. I took up my vigil, stroking his head, whispering, "O nobly born."

The inescapable leaving of color from the skin. How cool his fingers, though his arms were still a little bit warm, until they were not. Attendants took away the oxygen apparatus and he breathed quieter. We watched each breath and the long, long pause between, each gasp labored. His lungs were full. We could feel the gurgle. He was unshaven, unseeing, wide-mouthed, gaping radiance. This stark beauty of skin deep on bone. A thin coat.

Someone played the first line, "I have often walked, down this street before." I had my hands closest to him. There was no gasp or movement. There was not anything that stopped. His breath was just gone. At his neck, no tiny pulse. Out on the lines of the song, he went home. O nobly born.

3.

Coming home late in the night from Bruce, I find four blazing pictures of Angels in my inbox.

4.

I send a short email to a friend, telling about Bruce, including one of the Angel photos. Her reply:

Your Gift of Peaceful Passage

Thank you, Dear Bruce, whom I barely knew, for choosing this day to let go.
It was 45 years to the day that my father cried out to a stranger
wielding a knife, and died all alone.

The image of Jenny stroking your forehead, a crowd of friends singing and loving you,
gives me one more act of redemption, one more vision of peaceful surrender
one more weight on the balance
healing my heart.

Thank you for sharing the image and your experience of Bruce's passing.
They had much greater meaning for me than you could have known.
I felt your kiss in the wind . . . this message of the last breath, doors to worlds.

5.

Still on the same day, I hear a remarkable interview and transmission on blog radio. *Heavenly Blessings* is offering to all listening humanity the chance to be introduced to new levels of light frequency. Coming through my computer, I can experience profound levels of healing and cellular excitation.

In today's broadcast, the extremely versatile and genuine channel, Linda Dillon, brought through the Healers of Tralana and the Architects/Builders of Haleon. I had never heard of either of these populations of beings. I include a link to the site, so you can experience these transmissions for yourself.
http://www.blogtalkradio.com/inlight_radio/2012/05/03/heavenly-blessings

I have enough perception to see light moving and feel the effects. Everyone has these skill sets, whether active or latent. I believe we will all be able to perceive more broadly, more subtly, and of more refined matter in the coming times. Ultimately we will all be seeing more, feeling more, knowing more light.

What I experienced today was the intimate connection with the unknown audience also tuning in. I felt us as the collective and I understood that this is precisely how we do it, how we transform humanity.

Because Bruce had just passed, I was still in the awe of it. Daily I gave up the organization of my day to the Angels. I could see how they have arranged these days, this day, so that I could be healed and healer and carry the presence that is exactly needed now. A quiet alliance in loving service.

I used the example of today to show how the many levels of healing are operating—multi-dimensionally and across time. The Angels organized it all. I never knew of the Healers of Tralana. I was led to invoke them. Now I have experienced them. Now I know them as my allies. They asked to be invited and I took up the offer. Everyone benefits.

I will ask for the assistance of the Builders of Haleon. They are the builders of worlds. They built the pyramids and they built me, in a manner of speaking. I could perceive the sacred geometric shapes within my body as they flowed through the channel and out into my living room. (Amazing but true!)

That is what we need to learn about light—it goes anywhere, everywhere, instantly. Time is only a concept of the third density, which we are leaving. As our perception becomes more subtle, we will be able to see and know such wonderful things.

Oh lucky us that we get to experience all this crazy pain and loss and hurt and hunger. And birth and oceans with dolphins, the flowering dogwood, migrating birds, rushing rivers, shooting stars. What wild abundance of creatures and structures and particles of light.

One thing I add as my own reminder. When I pray, when I call for support from the Company of Heaven, I know enough to keep an eye out for a reply, because there will always be some reply. In some small way, some thing I could take as reply—a feeling, a nudge, a book laying open to a page, a synchronous word or phone conversation, a line of poetry come into my mind, a shaft of sunlight to hit a corner of beveled glass, exploding the whole room in diamonds. If my prayers are sincere, if my yearnings are from my heart and to the heart of One, something will turn and there will be an answer.

Perfect

I'm just beginning to get it. I cannot be perfect. I mean, I am perfect as myself, my particular expression of God. I am perfectly that and I am the only one who can be perfectly me.

But I cannot be perfection no matter how much my Virgo self tries. I cannot reach it. I cannot attain it. I cannot live perfection. Not in every moment, not in every action, not in every exchange. I wish I could and I chastise myself when I am not. But now I understand.

It's God's love that is filling me, it's the Angels of God who love me and come with me. They give me the words. They give me the eyes to see. They give me the words to speak in kindness and clarity of love.

I had been trying to get there on my own as a person, a woman no less. With humility I see that life's pummelings can break me or they can break me open. In that broken open, surrendered, but unafraid place the Angels can really inhabit me, fill me with their kindness and benevolent intent.

This takes all the phony pressure off of "me." All I do is surrender, which is not a cowardly action. It is in full trust and with some considerable joy that I let go of my need to be perfect. I see in a new way how arrogant living as part of the consumer machine has made us. Insisting that we could become better, near to perfect by driving a certain car or wearing a particular brand of jeans. How absurd. And sad, truly. That we have lost the knowing of how really perfect we already are, as who we are, not as God. Only God is God.

I know this from having a five-minute blast of energy from Andrew's heart this morning on the phone.

Not Always the Angel Lady

Sometimes I'm not the Angel Lady. Sometimes I'm barely a lady at all. When the old tone of voice of my mother starts spilling out of my mouth, I know I am in dangerous territory. This is no place for the faint of heart.

My mother had a terrifically strong voice with a great energy wallop behind it. Across a large room, she could bellow. As a child it was humiliating and could be quite dangerous if I didn't respond correctly. I believe I had to grow a voice to meet hers, otherwise I would be crushed and demolished. So my sharp voice reminds me from whence I came.

I may have spent years in silence in the ashram. I may have lived with Dorie, who loved me enough to take me into her family lineage. But I am by blood and DNA connected to my mother and her very potent voice. All my life I have attempted to respect the connection and soften the voice. But some days, that voice still bursts out of me. I know that spark is a part of sparkle. I am that. Flint of tongue on stone of hope. Dashed and thus flashed into spark.

A simple drive to the market, six stop signs and two speed bumps away. It can take seven minutes or twenty-five minutes. If someone does not know where they are or how to drive, that will be the person I get behind. It's bad. It's bad for me.

The person doesn't hear me in my car. He or she doesn't move faster or with more awareness. But, in deference to his ignorance or unawareness or both, I have entirely befouled my own air. I have yelled or sworn at him, useless though it may be. If a camera was snapped on my face then, I would not look anything like an Angel Lady. How far from perfect I am.

And you know what? The Angels love me anyway, tone of voice notwithstanding. When I come home from a foray into the wilds of commute-time traffic, I might write with the Angels about it. They are only loving. They might chide me sweetly and suggest good ways to think about the air around me and my thoughts too. I never feel unloved or reproached. I feel guided. I feel helped. I feel supported.

When I sit with them, I quite literally feel my entire being—body, soul, and mind—filled with unconditional love. This is how it is, every time. This gives me enormous comfort and quiets the negativity. Over time the Angels are helping me to love myself entirely.

I have a deal now with my Angels. I ask them to be in the back seat when I drive. If I see a trouble spot in the movement of traffic, if I feel that impatience rising, I reach behind me and feel an imaginal touch, a handshake, a high-five in the air.

> Thank you, my dear Angels, for helping me find some ease here. Thank you for showing me the birds who still flit from tree to tree, no matter what the traffic does. Thank you that I arrive in perfect time.
>
> Thank you for the grace and trust you help me to remember. I know these run through all my days. Thank you for your blessings right now.

Grace

Grace has been guiding me all along. I had no concept for that, so I had no frame to receive it consciously. My early home situation was brutal and terrifying for me. I felt I lived without any allies.

When I started meditating, I had a way to release some of the karmic demons through the process of "unstressing," releasing stress in the body through the long periods of meditation.

The graciousness of God is everywhere. I didn't know how to see it. Through the loving heart of Dorie, I was given some glimpses—or to say it another way—I was given different eyes. Angel Eyes, where everything is splendid. It is splendid just as it is. Every molecule. Every mote of dust. I believe this is the truth of existence in God's loving, expanding universe.

None of the old formalized religions dare to offer this wild love for the Divine and that the Divine has for us. It takes a truly wild divine One like Andrew to breathe it out with such splendid and stunning, rapturous exuberance that it can penetrate into people's hearts. He knows divine lovers and his love is fresh.

I have a different job to do, so I mustn't get caught in old self-doubt. Let Andrew polish me. Be honored in his gaze. Truly. Let him continue to open me to my own divine wildness.

There is another whole story for me and it is just beginning.

The Angels say, *Don't worry about a thing. We have guided you and you have followed well. Don't waste a moment regretting anything you didn't do. This is what you did—your life got you here in splendid lucid bliss and God's great shining love and glory.*

All of a sudden, on a Sunday evening, I see it is done. I am happy.

~ 10 April 2012
Easter Sunday
3 years after Kathleen's passing

Daily Life

One of the ways I get a visceral kind of confirmation that I am in the flow is when I go shopping. I don't have money right now, but I still get most everything I want. I go to a big Goodwill location called the Bargain Barn. It's an enormous old hangar filled with bins of clothes, household items, books, shoes. I like digging through stuff there. I like the loud, oldies music. I like the pigeons flying through.

I like the cashmere sweaters. I like the goose down comforters. I like the woolly slippers for me and for my guests. All my curtains were found there as well as my matching sheets and most of my towels. I have crystal vases and candlesticks. For my yard I've gotten wicker panels, a footstool, and a birdbath.

Going there is entertainment. And it's a way to tune in. Pay attention. Learn to listen with ease. I can't really make a bad decision there. The subtle perception is to listen, amidst the din. It's not a loud voice that says, "Look here." It's a little nudge. A persistent kind of leaning toward one bin or one side of a pile. Where to look. What to look for. What grabs my attention—color, texture, fabric. What interests me. When am I done. Pay attention.

When I come home with only a few things, I might think, "I didn't really find anything good today." But every single time I have treasures in my bag. A scarf I somehow grabbed at the last minute. Pants in a shade of sage exactly matching a top from last time, both in the finest Egyptian cotton. A pretty dish towel for my neighbor. A hand knit sweater for a new friend who lives over the hill.

I listen to my gut and often choose things I wouldn't normally get. Today I got a beautiful, berry bright sweater with great buttons for a friend who is going through a hard time. I think the gesture of giving, the quiet joy of it is actually more fun and more fulfilling than receiving. I feel good that I can be generous even without income.

So I don't really shop in stores anymore. This is always more fun and more rewarding. It's recycling. It's an adventure. It's ridiculously cheap at $1.25/pound. It's helping Goodwill. It keeps me humble. I am not ashamed; rather, I feel the abundance of the universe. I hold it in my hands. I see it in my daily life.

God Living in That Little House

Dear God of the Universe,

Are you living in that little chamber
inside me called my heart?

Are you twirling in the afternoon air
like the monarchs, flitting from tree
to tree, looking for the milkweed stem?

Am I the milkweed silk that you will weave?
Make me radiant like you are.
Make me shine.

When you were big and old and angry
like so many white men say,
I did not love you. Nor could I trust you.

But a power that lives and thrives
in the secret chambers of my heart—
well, that's a closer Friend

from whom I cannot turn away.
So I sit with you, invisible but tangible.
I make a fire and pour the tea.

I bless the rocks. I sing the stars.
I may be small, but this that lives inside me
makes the tiniest facets shine

and warms me through and through.
Smoke swirls up the chimney
for all to see.

Astonishment and Blessing

I laughed in astonishment this week. I wore a welder's helmet and saw the sun as a great green god in the sky who had a tiny fleck of Venus pass her face. I laughed in sheer joy as I saw for the first time this spectacle, viewed by millions, all looking up.

For the first time too I saw the graceful curve and twining of the pomegranate tree. She stood against a backdrop of granite boulders that were older than any of us looking. These moss-covered boulders made a long, deep hum of steadiness and wisdom when I listened with my arms around them.

The tree, her red flowers abundant in her bee-filled boughs, reminded me back to Rumi:

> Come to the orchard in spring.
> There is light and wine,
> and sweethearts in the pomegranate flowers.
> If you do not come, these do not matter.
> If you do come, these do not matter.

At the end of the Venus transit, the global meditation began. All the locations around the world were coordinated to this time. Opening our hearts and sitting together, 144,000 and more joined. I felt so much gratitude and calmness as breath and light united. The radiance streamed forth. An amazing wide peace emerged that went across everything. A great wave, coming together in unity and oneness. All connected to the whole, as One.

I was fully and subtly an active part of the collective. I put out a blessing and it was answered; I watched it go into everyone. Effulgence at my heart. The sanctuary doors were permanently open. Then the thought of Angels and, like a Blake etching, the Angels came down the pillars of Light. Rapturous, billowing Angels, luminous, within discrete textures of light. Everyone received this gentle, shimmering infusion on the lovelight energy of the collective.

I blessed one flower and the whole blossoming universe showered down.

Later the Angels wrote:

> Yes, dear One, we were blessing you in your fifth-dimension sight, your love sight. You saw the ladders of light, pillars, they sometimes say. You saw this light peopled by Angels, so you could have the sense of our multitudes. There is no end to the love in form that inflows to Gaia and her rising humanity now. You put that vision, that multitude into the collective consciousness. You saw the Angels of the Most High descending, arriving. That glory shall be yours—all of you—to see and know and live. You see why we say "Hallelujah!" Hallelujah indeed.
>
> Now is the time for steady growing faith, joy, and full disclosure of the hidden truths. Now is the time for insight to increase, for love to deepen and spread further through you.
>
> Send love and light as you do. Enjoy the flowering and know, indeed, what matters. Hold peace, love, and divine joy. Joy is the door now becoming your home. Treasure your precious self.
>
> We love you. We love you all and every One.

How I Came to Write This Book

I thought I knew quite a lot about Angels, from the close time with Dorie and the many kinds of study and experience. I spoke with them. I asked their help. I offered prayers and sent healings. Then came the opportunity to have Andrew Harvey stay at my house while he was teaching in Santa Cruz, and I was nervous. During my preparation, the Angels kept saying, "You don't know what will be the value. You are only thinking what a blessing for you that he will be here. But we tell you the benefit is for Andrew as much as for you, and for many more."

I made my house ready and he arrived, his self blazing at my door. Easily and smoothly, with hearts open, we met in this space. The Angels did healings with Andrew every afternoon. We talked of Dorie. He read her book. I saw the Angels surround him at his presentations.

One evening when he profoundly transmitted Rumi into the beautiful garden space we had prepared for him, all the audience felt the glory and the truth as it came out from him. At the end of the evening, but still in that expanded and rarefied state, Andrew turned to me and said, "I have seen hundreds and hundreds and hundreds of people. You are the real deal. You must write this book about the Angels." He saw and spoke the truth. It rang through me.

I could not rely on what I knew from the past. I had to open out the daily experience of living with Angels, here and now, to embody fully what I had learned.

So I began writing, uncertain in myself, but trusting in the Angels. Next to the towering brilliance of Andrew, I was even more nervous. I thought, "Am I worthy to do this?" I doubted whether I could do it. I doubted whether it could be done. I wrote my concerns and my fears. The Angels responded in such kindness and support, they soothed me of any lingering lack of self-esteem. I became more sure and comfortable in their communication. They were with me every day.

Since Andrew charged me with writing this book, I have done five things that have immeasurably deepened my days and made the writing a pleasure.

- start every day by giving the organizing of my day over to the Angels,
- align with the great I AM Presence; immerse myself in the Violet Transmuting Flame,
- say prayers of love and gratitude when I swim,
- pay attention when I am called to write with the Angels,
- stop listening to the regular news media.

As I continued, I knew even more deeply that the Angels loved me. I felt it pouring out of the energy stream of the words. My heart was filled by this love energy and my mind was soothed by the clean words they gave. I talked with them all the time, stating intentions and offering prayers. I thanked them for all the good that came every day. I sent them as light to places and people who were going through travail.

Their messages were simple and clear. They went right to the heart. Their love was unending. Their power was/is immense. Only good flowed from them in the pages. What I first experienced in a real way with Dorie was this steady, unwavering love. Now I felt it all the time from the Angels.

On Your Own

The Angels are helping me to be all that I am capable of being, serving the Light and honoring the beautiful love of Dorie.

These words, written in March 2012, confirm, reinforce, and support this book.

You are on your own but you are never alone. That is what you are learning now. Another level of release of an old story. It needed to be this much solitude for you to hear us so clearly. This is just how it is for you. Such a big, open, quiet space for you to download the light codes. Integrated through your bodymind, these light frequencies come out in the words and thought packets of the messages.

You are scribing the angelic realms down into the consciousness of light. Dorie brought in the first tangible vibrations, brought them down into mainstream. She made talking about Angels natural. She was such a noble and gentle soul, carrying true unconditional love.

Because you came to her so recently from the high purity and refined atmosphere of the ashram, you could immediately meet her, heart to heart. From the first moment to the last, that was true. No one can take that from your soul.

Now you expand that heart transmission out onto the page and the atmosphere.

The Direct Connection Is the Key to Human Transformation

When you establish a relationship with the Angels, they will open you up to the many blessings of the spirit, to the saints, mystics, other beings in other realms who do exist and are emanations of the Divine Light.

I include my stories and questions so you can see how much my Angels are with me, because they are my Angels and know me. They say, "No matter what you do, we are with you. Not like Big Brother. We see you with the eyes of a lover catching a sacred glance. That is how we feel about you. You are our person."

What I wish is that you discover *your* own Angels, that you be open to *your* angelic connections. Imagine how that will feel when your Angels are answering your particular questions.

The Angels are here, for everyone, waiting. Dorie was one of the first people in our time to bring the angelic vibration down here and walk amongst the people. She made it tangible; she made it easy. She opened up the possibility that we could live with our Angels and have our lives helped in so many ways.

Now all these years later, at this time of great transition, it seems perfect that this new energy flowing into us all—if we let it—is the fully enlivened, crystalline lovelight of the Angels and the Divine Source.

The completion of the Earth story unfolds by this grace and light. The Angels are real. The love and light they bring is grounded in the Earth by us. When we are participating in conscious light transmission, when we are in our joy, we are doing our job.

God placed His inextinguishable Flame of Love in you.
All the Light feeds the Flame.
The Flame and the Light are One.

I pray that you will find comfort, support, guidance, and most especially the truth of light in these pages.

May the Angels always bless you with their love.

Section 2

Writing the Book

Let Your Heart Open

Let your beautiful heart open.
Let it soar.
There is nothing like this smooth flight into Light.

Nowhere to go, but it seems you are moving.
Or it seems you are stuck, but still you fly.

Whenever you feel doubt, sit with us and explore it.
We go anywhere with you. Will you understand—we are your Angels.
It is our joy and our job to be with you, stay with you, support you, calm you, enable you, praise you.

You deserve all these things—as does everyone.
All humans have Angels, let there be no doubt.

Your frequency, your light resonance makes you a wonderful, open receiver.
Let this lovelight language move through you for the upliftment and betterment of the world.

You are not doing this. You are allowing it.
Let everything come out. We can edit later.

We love you.
We have always loved you.

~ 12 August 2011

This Book Is a Collaboration

This book will be a collaboration of us and Dorie and your good self. It will be a compendium of messages, exercises and a few poems, all lit through with radiance. You see, when we write with you, the words are interwoven with light. This light has the capacity to reach people through the page. Let this project happen. It will happen smoothly if you trust.

Can you feel how dropping down into your heart is the same as feeling us close around you? When you move into your heart, your mind stops agitating. When you move into your heart, your breath quiets. The expanse of your heart becomes apparent and available. Then, like a breeze lifting off from that lake, you can send love to a person or a place or a situation.

When you feel us, your many Angels around you, it is a familiar feeling of soft comfort. No effort. We just love you. You let this in and you soften. From this same place of ease and peace, we join you in imaging the whole world lit with light, covered with light. This will be the truth soon, and each mind imagining it helps to bring it to "reality."

Dear One, go forward now without fear and bathed in light. There is no greater service than you holding this frequency in ease and steadiness. We love you. We have always loved you.

~ 14 August 2011

The Writing

Dear One of the good heart,

This we tell you. The writing of this book, under the umbrella of Andrew's brilliance and support, is *for you.* You are a very bright One, and it is time for this light to be shining out. Your commitment to it is a recognition of this truth. Andrew saw the true strength of your light and rightly encouraged you. Again we say, *Do not be afraid. There is nothing to be afraid of.*

Your fears are old fears resurfacing to be felt in their terrible distortion of the truth and then vanquished. Use us every day to aid you in this release. You are correct. We have been with you all of your life. When you were the most in darkness, you had the habit of using your fine analytical mind to try to understand *why* it hurt so much. Now you know how unsuccessful that way of processing is. Now you know that calling on us, your own Angels, as well as the Archangels and the many Healing Angels who are available to you is the quickest, surest way to balance, peace, and freedom. In these last few days you have begun to realize this.

We are part of the "countless supply and never-ending prosperity of heaven," which are indeed yours. They are everyone's. You are a knower of reality and we are pleased to be working with you in this way. Continue.

~16 August 2011

This Connection with Angels

This connection with Angels—it's special but it's not unique.
Anyone can connect. Everyone does have an Angel or more than one around, waiting for assignment. You took this truth and colored your life with it.

Every silver streak of light, a thought strand of healing.
You saw these. You sent light. You sent prayers. You had prayer circles. You made prayer lists. You took the name in honor. You kept the pure vibration as Dorie did.

You invoke it now with the Violet Transmuting flame.

~27 August 2011

Notes on Receiving

This I take willingly and clearly.
Always I receive the words–
as they keep on flowing.
A certain kind of rumbling,
a buzzing, a live sound,
a certain pulsing, deepening.
Quieting. It's so still
while it is going on.

Dorie's First Greeting

Jenny love, it is beautiful to see you shine now with the fullness of this mission. You are so lovely and I love you so much. Doubt is false in this realm. Do not even go there. You knew me as Dorie, the someone who loved you and you loved. Now I am transmuting light down into the Earth.

I met and served so many people so that the first seeds of light could be planted. Now it is lovely to see them sparkling and opening in all those people. When they remember Dorie, that white-haired lady, they are comfortable in letting their hearts feel soft and in trusting people again. We have been working on this for a long, long time.

Now I want to bless all the people who will eventually read this book. I want to praise the ones who help you organize it and complete it. You don't know all of them yet, but this is a project of light and it is going forward beautifully.

Your high heart swells when you pray or bless. This raises your vibration. It raises the vibration of the whole field around you and extends out fifty or sixty feet. Beautiful, clear emanations.

Jenny love, we are completing a project we are meant to do. We might have done something then [when we were together in the 80s], but now you are ripe and the world needs the Angels so much. You are stronger now and there are no obstacles to our accomplishing something wonderful.

~8 September 2011

Beloved of the Angels

Our dear Jenny,

So many years ago Dorie called you *Beloved of the Angels*. She was right. Your pure heart attracts us. Do not be hard on yourself for the human/lineage feelings you feel. It is essentially impossible to live with a pure and open heart in the human environment at present. The world is making its choice, person by person, to go with the future of light or the old way of holding. The outcome is known, yet each One must make the choice. You chose early and you have been staying close to the truth in your heart. Never fear.

You loved wonderful people profoundly and they loved you back, even if they are gone now. We tell you there is never any love lost or wasted.

Your working with Andrew is utterly right and perfectly opening. This push is what was needed. What we delight in is the mutual benefit that is tangibly felt by you both. We bring the softening of power with the accelerating pace of peace that is rolling in on your world. Do not doubt that this is happening.

This more perfect self that you envision—it will be. The feeling of right-doing and strength from it—these are all indications of our support for you in this (ad)venture. The steady feeling of increasing goodness, subtle perceptions of shimmering light, waves of deep happiness—these are your signposts and guideposts; these are some of your confirmations. Wherever you feel *Yes* calling you or coming to you in the universe—that is the direction to select.

Swimming with prayer, love, and gratitude is a blessing for the whole environment. Keep doing it.

~8 September 2011

Transmission

My dear Angels,

I feel so happy and hopeful. I am at ease. Things seem to be going well. The magical numbers keep appearing to confirm the moment. I am glad to be here.

Thank you, my beautiful Angels. I love you. I love loving you. I receive your gracious love.

We, dear One, are also glad to be with you in this way. You are a very clear channel—of word and vibration. Meditation trained you well. The three foci, when accomplished and let go, allow this open mind. We put it another way. The training of mindfulness and meditation, the familiarity with silence, the subtle perceptions needed for discernment—make now for good transmission. The mind has been relaxed after much ability to focus. Relaxed awareness allows reception. As long as it keeps on flowing you keep on writing. When a word fails, the flow stops until what it is to be comes in. Very good.

Again, this means anybody can receive. The silence, familiarity, and insight here are excellent for clear, intricate transmission. You do not need to go elsewhere for confirmation, although we never stop you. You can get extra certainty.

The human population is starting to bubble up like sparkling water. The "spontaneous" gatherings, events, teleseminars, webinars, concerts, and worldwide meditations enhance the energy. Kindling is in place. Sparks are starting to fly.

~ 16 September 2011

Grounding Light

Dear Angels of my heart,

I love to sit with you. Is it better if I sit with you at the same time every session? What happens as we sit together?

Beautiful One,

We, too, love sitting with you. The connection/communication stream is instantaneous. We do not need to have sessions at a certain time or a regular time. Time is only a feature of your reality and we are always with you. Some others may find a regular schedule of sitting works for them. All such connections benefit the participants and the Earth.

You are receiving and grounding light in its particle form as it moves through your cells in its flow through to the Earth. At the same time, the energetic wave form ripples through you and out to all. The cetaceans are grounding light in the seas and you and others like you are grounding it on the land. Your scientists have much to learn about light.

Light is the power of the Divine. All healing can come in this way.

Equinox
~23 September 2011

Anytime

My dear Angels,

I feel best when I am writing with you or when I am reading the pages. Is this because it is me feeling my own vibration? And if I love it so much, how come I do not do it more often? (I can hear my mother's voice exactly in that loaded question.)

We love you, dear One. We love your openness and humor. There is time only in your world of duality, in your third dimension. The questions about time touch into core beliefs. But know we can meet you any "time."

This writing is in the flow, near to full flow, undistracted, pure-focused, peaceful, and in service. It must feel good. It should feel good. You are learning to follow indications, callings. It is not meant for you to write all day or even every day, if it is not feeling natural.

Let this writing be your meditation. If this smooth flowing through gives you calm and peaceful demeanor, then it's a good way to be with us.

Each time you let a sharp tone or feeling come up and release it, as here–asking for understanding–you are lessening the depth of the habit. You are softening the etheric vibration of disharmony. You are opening to an expanded experience of being human. Deep patterns are less in evidence by the work you do. Never despair. Be in peace. Good work is happening here.

We love you. Be at peace.

~27 September 2011

Big Enough

You have to know you are big enough to carry light. And then, of course, the more light you carry, the more light there is. You get lighter by admitting more light into your life. We speak as if it's a quantity, and it is in this way. Archangel Michael teaches that light magnetizes adamantine particles of sacred fire light to itself and adds to your light.

We call it clean love; no stickiness at all. Pure unconditional love. It is easy to send it out streaming, palms up, to each one you see. Often you have the thought sense of someone. When you send a love stream, a wave of bliss rolls over you. See yourself as a volcano of light, up flowing from the top of your head, rippling down, out over you and your world. This chair, this window, the stripes of the curtain interwoven with light.

Now you can also send healing through words, the printed words. The text can hold a vibration, even through innumerable printings. So it is thrilling to watch the light-filled work unfold–holding, sending, carrying, radiating ever-present, healing, loving light. Angel light. Divine light.

We call forth light in the printed word as a new vehicle for light. By the great love of the Angels, it is here in the lines. Let the light seep out through all the pages. Let light infuse every letter. Let light in, in this lovely, subtle way.

~ 18 August 2011

Trust

Every day we see hundreds of moments when trust is operating. That the sun will rise. That the lights will go on. That the car will start. So you all have the experience of simply trusting, automatically.

Your experience of giving your day over to us is a simple yet dynamic way to begin. Each time you ask for help or support from your Angels, guides, and the family of light, you allow the perfection of the universe to enter your daily life. Each instance of checking in, waiting a minute before taking action or speaking impulsively—each occurrence builds your trust.

One month of this simple starting practice will ground you in trust. And dear One, you cannot experience fear if you have found trust. Pay attention to inner feelings and knowings, as well as outside cues. Many people now notice the consistent sighting of 11:11 or 12:12 or 5:55. Magical number sequences that say, *Yes, you are right on track.*

These are small attunements. They add up to an expansion of trust. The readings of your heart's truth meter are strengthened and refined. The end result will be ongoing, widely pervasive, cumulatively increasing trust. All will benefit, especially you, the One who trusts.

~17 October 2011

Ready

Today is the day Andrew arrives for the second time. My house is ready. My heart is ready. A few more things to do to have what he likes. Now I ask for your wisdom and your blessings on this visit. Thank you.

Dear One,

We await with happy anticipation the return into your home of this great mind and heart, Andrew. He too is looking forward to seeing you and being in this "space" with you. He works tirelessly, for his mission is ringing clearly through him and calls to the deep-listening people. He looks for solid comfort, welcoming ease, and truth-speaking here in your abode. He does not look in vain. He sees you and the light you carry.

Can you speak about the pages I am ready to show him? What will his response be?

He's going to love them. You are correct; it is not the book he first imagined, but it is the book for the people and the call to put it together came out of your soul's purpose. You are on your mission by this receiving. It is a culmination of years of releasing and integrating. The old Worcester self could not have caught these words. So your own growth is underscored.

The book demonstrates trust and the release of your ego. The quiet purity of your home is the equal to the purity of the words, which have the capacity to touch people and draw them closer to their real home, inseparable from God. These clean words are "simple" because light is truth and cannot be complexified. It is precisely the right time and the unfolding will happen in a joyous and satisfying way. We are with you 100%. Throughout the pages our love for you is clear. Now that you know it without doubt, you have so much to offer. We are with you now, with so very much love.

~25 January 2012

Formed in Enduring Light

O my lovely Angels,

I see such a gorgeous and amazing unfolding as the book comes alive. The structure now is clear and your words are so kind and radiant. Have you something for me or us today? Thank you.

Dear One, who receives radiance,

You are well loved and now worthy to be pleased. It is good work. Your soul is shining, vitalized by being in this flow. We bless this venture. We bless the hearts and minds and skill sets that allow these transmissions to be received, organized, and presented for a wide audience.

We are and bless the pure vibration of lovelight that goes out in every page. The mechanics of such light transmission is not known because you must still think linearly. Nevertheless, it is going on. It will touch everyone who reads or hears the words.

Because we only speak truth and because you receive well the truth, the vibration of the book is solid. It has been formed in enduring light and this light it carries.

Soon enough we will meet you fully in the light. And yet our love for you then will be no greater than our love for your now or our love for you before you could even acknowledge us. The stream of love is unending, but oh the liveliness and fellowship of our meetings.

Be glad you have been born and have come to this time. Believe us and be clear—it *will* only get better.

~27 January 2012

Doubt

My dear Angels,

It's too simple. All the words are lovely and shining, but it's too simple. Are we just so much "la la" and "frou frou" of the New Age, which Andrew abhors?

Dear One,

He is such a powerful speaker, you do not want to raise his ire, but light is not "light" in action. It is not "lightweight" in its profound impact. That is the irony. The easier it gets, the lighter and smoother it gets, the more right it all feels—these are your indications to continue. These are the feelings we wish you to become accustomed to.

Your training as humans and participants in the grand illusion have stunted your innate perception of what is common and natural. It is the natural way for things to go well. But for now these thousands of years you have been so betrayed, ruled by corrupt leaders, and fooled into your own submission. So it is a reawakening just to imagine something of ease could be something going well, unfolding precisely as it should.

Dear One, your doubt is fine to be raised here. But it is not truth. Doubt has not produced the words or the prayers. Doubt has not allowed the inflowing of such light as has never been seen on the planet before this time. Doubt has not opened your radiant heart.

Light has done these things. So let light continue to add to your joy and your bounty. Let light continue to infill you and your work. Send light to Andrew. His work is stirring the collective pot. Yours is soothing it. The triumph of Light in your life is the object of all this. Trust it and the fullness of love engendered.

You are doing exactly what you must be doing right now. Invoking light, loving life, sending Angels, and being joyous in the experience. You are one of our strongholds of light, steady and reliable. Please keep on being this valuable resource to the forces of light and the Company of Heaven.

This message is for you. It is true. And we do love you.

~ 14 February 2012

Writing toward the Light

My dear Angels,

Can you help me move into the deeper layers of the book. How, by the telling, can some subtle experience be known by the readers?

Dear One,

We say it here. As you begin to write—as you formulate a question—you cannot any more turn down the dark road of fear or anxiety. You cannot even go there any more. As you write, you turn toward the light.

Show how easy it has become. That you start from a moment of prayer and joining. Then you write the first word. As that word is begun, the next word. And so it goes. The subtle turning is taking place in your mind/heart as the flow becomes steady and strong.

We have watched this many times with you. A mighty river cannot be turned around by a pebble. When you write it is a mighty river, and so the small old thought, the old stale tendencies to worry or fret cannot influence the flow. The flow of light is greater. It is the flow of truth. Be in this truth.

~26 April 2012

I Am Not Empty

I am not empty when it is done.
I am full.

I am so full.
I am not even here.

Section 3

Who Are the Angels? The Fundamental Message of the Angels

A New Day on Earth

Today literally is a new day on Earth.
There has never been so much light beaming onto Earth.
The people are awakening in vast numbers.
They also are aware of their Angels, so the light quotient is like never before.
It is thrilling to see and be a part of.

Now as you go through this day—which you have already given over to us to organize—watch this unfold to give you confidence in the process.

Watch that your heart is lighter.
Watch how it feels as you drive. Is it smoother? Are you less combative in your thoughts?
Watch as you greet people. Is your heart open and loving?
Watch as your energy remains steady and strong.
Watch as feelings of joy arise, sometimes from nothing.
Watch as those familiar flashes of spinning light are seen just at your edge of vision.

These things remind you and confirm your alignment.

From our side we see this happening as waves of light traverse the globe. In the same way as waves of your ocean intercept and cross and roll over each other, so too these individual waves of light are washing over the planet.

They are literally washing over your third-dimensional awareness. This is part of the cleansing. It is happening everywhere, every day. For you, dear One, it is happening here in your life and fully in your heart.

Go in peace. We love you.

~ 13 August 2011

What Is the Role of the Angels, Especially in These Times?

This is a good time. This is what we came for, what we wait for. This is what you are ready to contain, transduce. Let the light come in!

We are the living light in personified packages according to the need. We are as close to the Pure Source, which is Love. Some say Christed Light. This Divine Light inhabits us into what can be called individuation. So we can appear as appropriately-sized helpers on the road or messengers with wings.

From the beginning of time, there have been Angels in the universe. Now they await the invitation into your life.

~15 August 2011

Inseparable

My dear Angels,

Thank you for being with me so much more strongly. I can feel you in the workings out of my day and my life. Today when I was at the pool getting ready for my laps, I felt light lifting off my skin. A fluid vibrancy is around me. I see people seeing it.

Maybe because I smile, it makes it OK for people to look at me and catch sight of the light. I am happy in this introductory capacity—just let them see a bit more light and feel good about it.

Dear One,

How could anyone be afraid of the Light? The illusion placed that seed of fear in humanity a long time ago. The power elite of the churches made God so formidable, so fearful. Made people afraid to even think they could have a personal relationship with All That Is. Now you find, each day, more clearly, your inseparable connection with God.

Such is the truth you carry when you spread light.

~23 August 2011

Seeing Angels

I love you, my dear Angels. Will I ever see you?

Good Evening, dear One,

You will see us when your perception is refined enough for that to be an all-time reality. You are sensing us already and have been doing this naturally all your life. Do not doubt what you know to be true.

Remind the people that there are many kinds of sensing. You can feel us in the breeze. You can smell a subtle, sweet fragrance when no flower is near. Some people notice pulsing or flashing light in their peripheral vision. Some feel a light touch on their shoulder, like the hand of a dear friend. Whatever you notice, it will feel comfortable. It will feel safe. It will feel loving. For that is what we do. We love you, each and all.

~1 September 2011

Light Is Essential

Light is essential,
so you must know you can receive light.

You are already receiving light daily.

Learning to experience
It * Yourself * Presence
 * Light *
is the door and the thing
experienced.
That's why it is a wave and a particle.

This is the refreshment of the senses.
Light pouring through
as sound or feeling or insight.
All food.

Hype

We let the hype about the Angels in the 80s and 90s work for us. All that attention, those images, the rapidity with which it came into prominence showed us that people were interested. They wanted it to be true. And, of course, it was true. But the media and the advertising executives took that beautiful curiosity and bombarded everyone. It was a perfect way to make piles of personal money and jade the public perception. Think of the people like a field that has been plowed and sown with legumes. Now the soil is rich and stable. Now the real and necessary truth about the Angels can come out.

Many sources now say, *Call on your Angels and guides.* These words become familiar. And our great Saint Germaine and the Violet Transmuting flame burns away the old, the dross, the resistance. This is the most exciting time.

We want all the people to know how near their Angels are. We wish that every person could say, *Hello, my Angel. Won't you come fully into my life now? I ask for your help, support, and guidance.* It's that simple. The most amazing and profound things can happen. If everyone said that or thought that, we could come into the world and change things "in the twinkling of an eye." It is not hard. Solutions already exist. Putting many things together and dismantling other operations could change the entire state of affairs.

~8 September 2011

Be Calm

Dear One,

Be calm and steady in your daily life. Things on every level are transforming. Your cells are integrating very high frequencies of light so that you will be able to function flawlessly in the higher dimensions. Things are going well if you do not listen to the news. The media is one of the last strongholds of the dark forces, so it is best to just let them wither away by taking your attention entirely away from them.

There is a separation going on. Those many, many millions who will go each day a little more towards the light. Their lives will continue to transform as the energy in which they live is changing, refining. Those who are still choosing to live in the bowels of greed and despotism, no matter how distinguished on the face of it, they may continue, but not for long. With each One coming more into the fullness of Light/Love/God, the intensity of the light cannot be misunderstood. The time of the dark is over. These are the death throes. It is an ugly and rancid beast and the stench will be around for a while longer. But the reach of this "hungry beast" is lessening every day. Be steadfast.

Your own machinations, dear One, are the workings out of very old human ways. A robust spirit in a body limited by time and circumstance creates a flashpoint, a flint. You flare. You do not do great harm, but your sting is potent. You could be happier with the outcome of your interactions, and there would be no residue of disappointment the next day.

First be aware and then be grateful that you pay attention to feel the sting. The impulse to snap comes quickly. That is your moment. We will help you to be more aware then. That is the power point. Your great light will be served by the continual softening of this irritation. Like a cooling balm applied to inflamed cells, we apply the cooling ointment of clear seeing. You are loved.

~ 12 September 2011

Advice for the Humans

Today we have some simple advice for you all.

• Begin to wean yourselves of the news media.
The scheduling of meals and news consumption together lowers the vibration. Parts of you are triggered and then fear has you. In these moments, call on us most specifically. *Thank you, Angels for showing me something better to do or think.*

Use the news "information" to know where to send light. Sometimes the only truth in the news stories is the location. Sometimes even that is created to produce a specific effect. Listen with discernment.

• Practice sending and receiving.
The more you call in the Angels, the more you ask for counsel or comfort or support, the more the light around and in you intensifies in your life. More of you is being transmuted into a lighter body. You may not notice it yet, but subtle body processes are now being powered by light energy.

As this inner light technology becomes more pervasive in your own body and in the mass consciousness, malformation will disappear. All handicaps of body genetics will be cleared from human consciousness.

These are the waves that are engulfing the planet. So begin with sending light. If you do not know or care for the situation, send light to the Angel of that place. This is very helpful and effective in lessening tension in old villages. It is felt as blessing from the ancestors, however the particular culture imagines that. The blessings come from the realm of light.

People getting accustomed to sending light is a way to directly lessen tension—in yourself and in the other location. This is an action which only produces good. Send light.

After a while you realize you must be light to send it. And so the possibility of seeing your own self as light begins to emerge in your consciousness.

Some people have very clear, very strong, direct experiences when they consciously send light. Some people need slow, steady exposure to the idea. All people end up being happier and more content when angelic help is accepted as natural and very much deserved.

So you send light out to a place or person or situation. Sending light to the Angel of the place is always beneficial. And we send light to you. Knowing this can be and is operating in your life allows for more confirmation.

We really only love you.

~23 September 2011

The Question of Angels

My dear Angels,

What reply would you give to the question: *What do we really know about Angels?*

We are so pleased the question of Angels is arising again on people's lips. Of course, we have always been with you, but now more people are knowing this is true. And more people are quietly wondering, hoping those stories they heard and felt as children are true. They are true—if the seed of the story is that each person has a Guardian Angel. This is absolutely true. Each person is given a Guardian Angel at birth. That Angel is with you always. Many people have more than one Angel, but everyone has at least one.

Your Angel's job is looking after you. Your Guardian Angel's joy is bringing into your life things and encounters that help you have your dreams come true. These are simple words which cover a multitude of actions.

Discussions about how many Angels can sit on the head of a pin as well as discourses on levels and principalities and the like are distractions presented by those who want to make you believe you could not be worthy of knowing, closely knowing the Angels. Hierarchies do not exist in the angelic realm. We have different foci, but no Angel is better or more important than another. This is not possible.

~3 October 2011

Human Angels

Dear Angels,

Are there human Angels?

Yes, dear One,

Humans can be moved to take actions which are guided by the Angels. In some circumstances an Angel cannot materialize; it would not be for the good of the people concerned. A human Angel can be moved then to take a human action to help the one in need.

Help comes in so many forms. This will be one of the many revelations that you will see in your world. When you ask, help is immediately with you in seen and unseen ways. Your own discernment will guide you.

~ 19 October 2011

We Are Creator's Pure Spark

My dear Angels,

So much beautiful love when I feel you now, when I think how wide the reach of your love is. I see and feel how you are the light gates closest to us.

Dear One,

We love your reverie and receptivity. We surround you in light even as we are light. We are light. We are Creator's pure spark in a form conversant with humans. We are one of the ways to see God (to use your Old Testament vocabulary). We are a way to feel loved, something nearly all humans need to learn. We can do so much for you, but you must ask.

We understand that for many, the idea of someone always being with them might be more off-putting than comforting. We understand that a feeling of embarrassment could arise. We understand how your mistaken feelings of unworthiness could block your receptivity.

Happily none of these false idea streams can ever influence our love for you.

~26 October 2011

A Lifelong Resource

The Angels are part of any human endeavor. They are the closest thing to you, having been with you since your first full breath. This is not to say the angelic kingdom has not been with the soul through gestation, only that your own particular Guardian Angel is called to you as that breath is breathed out and in. From then on, the love and joy and the job of this Angel is you. A lifelong resource of comfort, sustenance, support, magical happenings, and elegant, perfect timing. In a word, your Angel.

The illusion has allowed this tender and gracious companion of constant support to be diminished by some religions, enlarged in terrifying ways by others, ignored by still others. Yet we are deeply known in all indigenous teachings. Peoples who know ancient truths know spirits are with them. Carrying the power of the Creator, directly and personally, loving you without reservation, without condition. Love only.

Your Angel, if you let it, can enliven in you the real experience of unconditional love. Never-ending. Always there for you. The more you cognize this enormously graceful force of love for you, the more you become it. You become a human carrier of Divine love and light. The Angels are the most personal entry to this realm.

Because illusion presents everything in contrast, the truth of the Angels got stratified. There is nothing of hierarchy in our realm. Every presentation that suggests "better," "bigger," "more important," "more powerful," "more beautiful," "more valuable," "holier," is at least tinged by illusion. There is no hierarchy in Oneness. It is a false idea from limited mind.

Once you cognize or "grok" how unendingly your Angels love you, you will experience it, know it, find yourself alive in that love. Let it inspire you.

The Angel's job is to keep the flame of the Creator's pure love lit in you. However small the flame, it cannot be extinguished.

The Angel is indistinguishable from the inextinguishable light of God within you. This is the first stage of Self-Realization—to see yourself as receiver of the flame; see the Angels as keeper of the flame; igniter of others by this flame.

~26 October 2011

Now You Know

My dear Beautiful Angels,

Can you say some words right now? No questions, but the quiet, instant connection that feels so fine. Thank you!

Dear One,

We perceive you getting used to the idea that we really are with you all the "time" with no sense of intrusion and absolutely no judgment. You get used to feeling support and comfort and confirmation. These are important qualities for you at this time. You will be called to teach and help in leading the great mass of humanity to its light-filled destiny. So your personal doubts and especially your experiences of bliss, love, and glorious connection are very important—to you and to them.

Your openness is a blessing. You influence others by this quietly expanding field of acceptance. Your friends look to you for new information, and we are thrilled you begin to know that your family of light is quite near.

Now you know. You cannot go back to before. There is only now and now you know. We love you.

~6 November 2011

Not Earth-Shattering

Dear Angels,

I wake from a dream where I tell a friend that this book is not earth shattering. You say with a smile, "No. Our intention is not to shatter the Earth. It is to raise the vibration so you can live in the paradise that Earth is."

What message do you have for me today, my dear Angels? I am feeling untethered and drifting.

Dear One,

We wish you to be learning each day that we and many other beings from the Company of Heaven are actually by your side. Because you cannot fully see us with your limited vision, you let yourself fall into the untruth that you are alone. You are not alone. You are never alone. Those instances when you sensed us with you/above you in the clear pool where you swim—they are true. You sense us then more easily because you are at ease and happy when you swim. If you were to feel that smooth and centered at other times, you might recognize us. That was not a reproach. All of your unfolding is our unfolding into you as well. And so we iterate all goes well, dear One. Your mind is opening beautifully supported by your widely opening heart. Bless you. Be steadfast in these last days of the old. It is tight. Birth is on.

~ 19 November 2011

General Upliftment

My beautiful Angels,

It felt like you called me, arranging a rendezvous, Ooh la la! I am here. Thank you.

Dear One,

Our beautiful One, whom we love. You are realizing this gift of cognitive sight and comprehension while viscerally (aurally) receiving. Now the channel is clear. Let us begin.

You are in a phase of extraordinary development. All forces are at play. We do not wish to imply distress or concern, but the awareness of the greatness of the wheel that is turning, to use your words. The vast heart of God in each of you begins to resonate together, across what were once boundaries—self, Earth, Company of Light.

There is general upliftment. The wave is rising and you are going with it with ease and grace. Water lifts you easily so you feel it as something familiar. There is nothing to fear.

Feel comfortable in your knowing. This ease is so important now. You will be a steady torch when the old lights dim. It will not be the three days of darkness as some have said. That was then. Now the rising awareness across populations, across generations, across species. We see an increase of light that is stunning. All of everything you have done has brought you here, each of you.

We are coming together. We truly can say, *See you soon.*

~23 November 2011

You Will Truly Be Amazed

Each life is so unique. When you finally see all that you are and all that you have come through, you will be truly amazed at yourselves. Each of you is creating your life out of unlimited options. It may not seem like that now, but soon you will see in a very clear way how in each decision, even ones not conscious enough to be recognized as such, you yourself chose the feeling, the intensity and length of its occurrence, the thoughts surrounding it, and the next likely action. You are weaving the cloth of your life with every movement of your fingers.

Full consciousness will reveal the complexity and enormous beauty that you are in this universe. We are so eager to sit with you and exchange understandings. So much will be apparent to you once you are free of the limitations of third density. It will be glorious for us to sit with you and see the comprehension spread across your face.

~28 November 2011

Fulfilling Your Purpose

Dear One,

As we see you waken in calmness and gratitude, you truly are demonstrating the changes in a human psyche as it moves into full consciousness. We are encoding vibrations in you from the highest dimensions. This is what you notice just as you are waking. Your trust and openness allow easy infusion and smooth assimilation. It is your job to then walk out into the day integrating the incremental steps of your new awareness. The quality of life you have, the quietness, the uninterrupted hours, allow you to notice the small ways that change. You are catching yourself immediately after any traffic-related outburst. (Smile. We love you.)

When you are fulfilling an essential piece of your purpose as an inhabitant of Earth, there is peace and contentment. The drive to do is diminished as the quality of being grows. If you stayed in your room all day simply breathing in and out, appreciating the changing light, allowing us and the light to flow through you, you would be contributing to the New Earth. Your peace makes a corridor of peace, an arena for this frequency to ripple and stir, an area that can be seen because of its quiet, steady shine.

We see you. You will see your family of light so very soon.

We love the space of grace. Be wildly happy in your human existence, as it wraps up this extraordinary phase of transformation. Hold on to your seats. Be not afraid. We bless you. We love you.

~ 16 December 2011

The Unstoppable Entry of Lovelight

We are very pleased that you truly, TRULY, now know and believe fantastic things are coming into your reality. You are coming into your own on a higher octave. You assimilate new light data increasingly faster and smoother. New knowledge, comprehension, and compassion grow in you.

Your role is to offer acceptance to all. People trust you in these matters. Now get ready, for you are going to shine.

By seeing the light in you, people begin to think it could be true and they could have it too.

Dorie says:

Everything we said about the Angels is true.
Now it is backed by the whole Company of Light.
Their intervention in your lives is at the Creator's will.
The unstoppable entry of lovelight into your bodies and your planet is guided by their grace.

~25 December 2011

Receive the Light

My dear Angels,

Thank you for being now so woven through the fabric of my life. What is your instruction today?

Receive the light. Do not doubt your mission or the truth of the inflowing light. Your body and consciousness are in dynamic change now. The slightest fluctuations of the mind stuff send out tangible ripples. If the mind fluctuations entrain with the heart, then beautiful waves of calm emanate. In groups this is magnified, amplifying the harmonic.

This is of the highest importance and for the good of all. Thus swimming in the pool where these emanations move smoothly out is excellent for you, as a strong sender, and for all those who receive this extra energy in the form of lovelight through water.

Receive the light. The same instruction for you and for all the people. All are One.

~7 February 2012

Seeing the Self as Light

The Self gets used to seeing itself as light. This is the change that is happening. You become more at ease, familiar in a strange marvelous way with yourself as a light being, someone who has a light body. This is who you primarily are—and have been for the whole of your incarnations into matter. This light being chose to clothe itself in bodies of other maturations and densities so it could inhabit other places and experience other kinds of lives. Always, inside you knew you were of light, made of light.

The ego takes the "I" from I AM. It thinks it does things, takes action. The only real actions are done by the I AM through the heart and mind and focus.

You are soon to be living in an incredibly diverse light world. This will happen as more people turn from judging things they don't like or want or are angry about and instead focus on the positive and radiant things their deepest self desires for themselves and the world.

The ego is the narrator of its own story. When the soul's purpose is not being met, the ego begins to try to organize things to favor it over another being.

The ego must fail because the coat cannot run the body; it can only cloak it. The body and the soul and the mind and the talents all want to fulfill the soul's purpose.

This dampening down with false limitations has made the Self doubt its intrinsic value. Always remember the Self is of God. The Creator. Each One is That.

That's how it was supposed to be. Now your transformation into exactly that is assured.

~Christmas Day, 2011

Light of the Mother

My beautiful Angels,

What is the particular relationship between the Mother and the Angels?

Dear One,

Divine Mother is the Carrier of Bliss. She is Queen of Heaven. For her compassionate heart, She is revered. She is the Answerer of the supplicants. She hears the prayers of the ill and the forgotten. She appears to children who know the truth inside religion. Mother of the World, She holds Creation, its creatures, the hearts of the innocents in her vast domain. Her love is comforting and it is nurturing. She receives all. She is Quan Yin, returned until every soul is back in the light. Her reign is eternal.

We, the Angels, do the work of Light in her realm. She moves through the world in vast sweeps of compassion, forgiveness, and unconditional love. Her love gave vision to the great leaders of peace and truth. Her light is noble, resplendent, and extravagant.

You could say we work for Her when we work with you. When you speak to your Angels, you are receiving Her grace.

If you live in a country, you are part of the life of the monarch whether you ever meet and bow. This is a poor analogy, but on Earth you know only hierarchy. In the realms of Light, there are levels of light, densities, but not rulers. Each one is where the energy register is compatible. In light you cannot be "out of line" or "out of place."

So you are in Her realm by your existence. If you turn to Her, you can be in Her embrace, in Her heart—the Heart of Compassion, Wisdom, Tender Mercy.

We, the Angels, by our presence in your lives, build your container of light. When you take us into your trust, when you speak to us, when you ask for guidance and support, your hard edges soften. Activities and thoughts of denser vibration fall away.

Your life in its increasing joy and fullness demonstrates the "in the moment" rewards for living with the Angels—especially now. Intermingling your life stream with your Angels opens you into the Divine Mother. We are not the only way, we are not the necessary way, but we are quite often the Ones who take you into Her chamber, Her garden, the lake of Her luminous embrace.

There is no divergence here. The blessed radiance of Her gaze beholds all in its true unity: Bliss.

The Light of the Mother is Divine Grace. She is the true lover of each and all, in their thought of individuality—each human, each creature, each universe, and each fragment of pure Source essence that you call Angels.

It is Her love that infuses your world. There are numerous embodiments of the Mother so that different cultures can enjoy the blessings of Her physical Presence and Her luminous grace. The world is in need of these limitless reservoirs of Love, from which all can draw sustenance.

As Queen of Heaven, She is Queen of the Angels. The realm of heaven is not stratified. She is loved by all and revered without end.

~8 February 2012

Meditation with the Mother

The most powerful force in the universe is the force of the Motherhood of God, the radiant love force that is streaming from the light and creating everything.

Imagine the Mother above your head in whatever form you imagine Her.
Imagine Her surrounded by golden light.
Imagine that light pouring from Her hands
down through your skull,
turning your brain to gold.

Imagine it opening your third eye in the middle of your forehead
and opening that,
so that it radiates like a diamond.

Imagine it pouring down into your throat.
How beautiful, that gold light pouring from the Mother.

Imagine it opening the center in your throat, that red rose center in your throat.
So that red rose opens like a fragrant, pungent flower.

Imagine the light now going down into your heart,
washing away all the clouds around your heart
so that your heart blazes like a sun.
So that the gold light is pouring down, down, down,
because love flows down, love flows down.

And your brain is a golden brain,
and your eye is a diamond eye,
and your throat is a rich, red rose opening,
and your heart is a blazing sun.

And now take that light down.
Let Her pour that down into your stomach,
so your whole belly center becomes a massive heap of golden wheat,
a rich heap of golden wheat, pungent and beautiful.
You can feel its balance and its richness at the core of yourself.

And take that light down to the bottom of your feet,
and give up all the struggles and pains and agonies of your past lives
and give it up to Her healing power.

And now the whole of you: body, heart, mind, and soul,
genitals, and spirit—all of you, all of you, is infused by the golden light of the Mother.

And very humbly but very grandly and very deeply and richly
you now know that you are the child of the Father/Mother.
You are the embodied Divine child.
You are a drop of the ocean of Divine Presence.

And now knowing who you really are, make a dangerous vow.
Make a vow to really face where we are.

Ask for the courage to have your heart broken.
and to have your true, radical, heart-broken mission revealed to you.

So that you can go out armed with this joy and matured by the grief
to become a Sacred Activist and to change this planet now.

All hail and praise to the Divine Mother,
who, despite all we do, continues to love and infuse us with Her grace.

~*Meditation by Andrew Harvey. Used with his gracious permission.*

Be Glad You Are Aware of the Miraculous

My dear Angels,

I write today's date at the beginning of this new year with amazement. This is the 28th anniversary of Dorie's passing. I remember it so well.

Precious One,

We greet you in this new year with love and honor. Our gratitude is with you for writing these words for the people. You allow this flow to enrich and inspire. Yes, we are always with you. We know you live now in a deeper knowing regarding our existence, our nearness, our power to bring the miraculous into your life. Because, dear One, a miracle is something you cannot explain by ordinary means; much of what we are able to do in your daily lives is outside the ordinary—even if it is simply holding a traffic signal green, setting up the circumstances for an auspicious meeting, inflowing light into the receptive heart.

Be glad you are now aware of the miraculous and can write these words for the people. Be glad for your heart and your life. Be glad.

We tell you your meeting Dorie was part of your soul contract. Writing now as you do is a fulfillment of that contract. And it will continue. Your own "gentling" toward yourself is the model as well as the proof. Remember, in the individual life is where the soul's growth and advancement are most purely seen. You may take actions that reach the multitudes, but your greatest good is re-learning, remembering your God Self, your true heart; living connected to Source. In this way light and unconditional love radiate out from you. These qualities reside in your home. This is part of the welcome and comfort people feel when they enter. This you learned from Dorie. She is glad it continues here.

~4 January 2012

Transforming Our Bodies

My dear Angels,

Andrew asks, "How does coming into consciousness with our Angels transform our bodies? We have been told a great birth of an embodied Divine humanity is the evolutionary destiny of humanity. What is the role of the Angels in this great birth?"

Thank you for your blessings and your gracious understanding.

Dear One,

You are correct, dear Andrew, it is the same question. When the angelic beings, Ones from the angelic realm are fully invited, consciously embraced in a human life, the quality of that person's life immediately begins to change. It used to occur slowly; now the old timelines do not apply. You will never go back to that protracted and habitual functioning. The time for slow growth is past.

So including the Angels in your thoughts and prayers, in your consciousness, is more like eating light. The Angel's constancy is a portion of the food you and your body hunger for.

The Great Central Sun and our many allies from the star nations have been pouring light upon Earth. The cetaceans are grounding this light in the oceans. You, as awakening humans, are grounding light into your mother Earth. This is very important.

Once your Angel is allowed entry by you into your energetic field, your Angel, who knows you so well, is able to keenly direct the light as it enters your physical body. Dorie says it this way, *You don't think. You just accept, as the Angel pours the great healing light into every part of you.*

The subtle energy channels are infused with light. Your cells transform so the structures become crystalline. It is impossible to operate in a rigid or habitual way. You can only be flexible, humble, and grateful, as you cook, cook, cook. Do not be afraid. This is what we all have been waiting for.

Imagine our love when we are able to infuse and direct these healing flows in each of your bodies, in precisely the way to heal you completely and bring you to full consciousness.

As each individual says yes—out loud, in a whisper, in a thought, in the heart space—the fullness comes. Then you will see that you have all finally and at last said Yes. This is the New Earth rising.

The Company of Heaven says, *Our sacred purpose is to unfold the Divine Plan through physicality.*

~1 March 2012

Relationship with a Human

Dear Angels,

Andrew asks you, "What does the relationship with a human give to you?"

Thank you always.

Dear One,

It is our joy to be invited deeply into your life and thought. It is also our job, our only job at this time. We learn how you operate, your modes and moods, so that we can assist you in every kind of task and understanding. We are your conduit to most anything you could want. The fulfillment of desire comes from fullness of heart. We help you, each of you, to trust your heart, to trust love. Trust that you are loved—by your Angel as well as the many great beings who are involved with the Earth now.

You are here for a reason and your Angels and guides are with you on your mission. In many cases, a sense of your Angel is the first instance wherein a person feels this sense of mission. So communication with us opens the gateways.

Everything comes from Source/Creator God. We transmit into your particular life what is aligned with your mission, the Divine Plan for you—if you let us. You may stumble around, but you do not need to stumble and fall.

If you do invite us in, share with us your dreams and your sorrows, we can assist you enormously. We *are* with you. Knowing this without doubt would relieve so much misery.

We are the spark of Source that remains pure while intermingling with you. We have no motive or need. We are your protector, your guardian, your lover, your friend.

With you in your certainty—call it trust—and your Angels in their constancy—this is invincibility.

The more you are in your true service, aligned with the Divine Plan for your life, your Angels are in their most exquisite joy.

~3 March 2012

Section 4

How I Work with the Angels: A Guide into the Healing Practices

The Invitation Is So Big

The invitation is so big.
It is given to each of you, individually.
It is personally delivered. God-filled.
Inspired by all the threads of goodness
that you have ever woven of your life.
Now is the time. Come.
The door is open. It is your heart.

Keep Your Attention Easily with the Angels

The work is to keep your attention easily with the Angels, open to the possibility of miracles and unknown happenings. Dorie says, *the impossible is possible.* Your attention, the focus of your mind, which draws the fullness of your heart—these things must be with the Angels.

This may be the gap, the silver place between the worlds, the crack in the cosmic egg that allows you to transcend, go beyond the seen worlds to the core of reality at its unseen, unmanifest form.

The full unmanifest, the Absolute, does not come out into form; the Angels, the first light sproutings of the manifest, show themselves, but in such subtle ways that your usual third-dimensional eyes cannot see them.

Is this the same as practicing the presence of God? God has seemed so big and far away. Your own Angel, who loves you so much, who has never been known to fail, in whatever you ask, this Angel, these Angels, are so easy to call. All it takes is your attention. It's like being in prayer all the time, only not disconnected. You do not have to go anywhere to call the Angels; you do not have to leave, even for a moment, where you are. You only have to let your attention quiet, fall into the lively, silent gap, and ask.

Your Angels are there even as you start to think of asking.
With the thought of Angels, they are. The poet Rumi says,

> *Lo, I am with you always,* means when you look for God,
> God is in the look of your eyes,
> in the thought of looking, nearer to you than yourself,
> or things that have happened to you.
> There is no need to go outside.
> Be melting snow.
> Wash yourself of yourself.

~24 August 2011

Report

Each day, as soon as I wake, before opening my eyes, I give my day over to you, my Angels, to organize. Then I ask to be aligned with the Divine Plan for my life, the Divine Plan for Gaia and all who inhabit her. May all sentient beings live this day in grace.

Now that I am paying attention more, unwanted explosive thoughts have not arisen. Anger has not significantly arisen, especially now that I do not listen to the news. I am not an ostrich; I send Angels to the places of conflict.

I anchor in light with every conscious breath. I allow the Angels to guide me. I am receiving more communications from the other realms. These purer beings speak inside my head. As long as I keep writing, the words keep coming. I trust this. I have always trusted it. I have not been led astray.

Lots of times I didn't ask, didn't pray, didn't stop and wait. Lots of times I've made bad decisions. But it seems every time I have taken the time to find quiet inside and then asked a question of my Angel or asked for help, a good thing has happened. And usually in a good, smooth, right-feeling, non-resistant, natural way.

I am again reminded of Dorie saying, *When the timing is perfect, you know it's Angels.*

Yes, that is all true. But paying attention makes it more so. Paying attention to the slight flickers of light at my back or just at the edge of my peripheral vision allows me to sense more around me. I feel my inner sight becoming more refined. The sense of something on a most subtle level is very vibrant.

~31 August 2011

Use Your Skills. Use Your Life.

Dear Angels,

Is there a message you have for me or for the people today?

Dear beloved One,

We see that although you believe we are always with you and that we always love you, you let an old habit of first thoughts speak themselves each day. You wake up. You align yourself with spirit. But then as you get up, you speak out from an old grumbling mind. No one else hears it, but you lower your vibration by this. So we guide you to say something more clearly affirming. Perhaps, *I am ready to begin a new day. My heart is eager for the day to unfold because I have already given it over to you, my dear Angels.* Now doesn't that feel better?

Beloved One, you have so many skills and resources. You truly have been waiting for this time for your whole lifetime. And be assured that your previous lifetimes were also in service to this time. There is nothing to fear.

So use your talents. Use your skills. Use your perceptions. Use your heart. Use your words. Use your life, right now, so that this day, this very question you asked will affirm and confirm your unalterable connection to us, to spirit, to the Godhead and the Source. All is One. We love you. Be at peace.

~4 September 2011

Nervousness and Anxiety

Dear Angels,

I feel nervous and anxious within a few minutes of hearing the daily news . . . and the stock market. Am I being naïve and foolishly optimistic to think and tell others you can do so much; you can help us in so many ways. Thank you, dear Angels, for speaking truth to me and helping me understand.

Bless your heart, dear One,

We love you. We appreciate these feelings that come up when you hear news stories—even if the stories are about past deeds and current legal action.

You are stunned again by the depravity of people who are your leaders, and the soldiers who carry out their orders. When people are afraid, they let down their moral guard and take actions that can only be seen as unconscionable. To these people, send light.

Send light to the victims and their families. Send light to the old lands heavy with blood and negativity. Send light if you can even to the hearts of the old leaders. They knew what they were doing. Their karma and life review will be as keen and precise in painful overview as the events were for their victims. But that is for them to experience.

For you, the purpose is to feel the turning to light with all your needs and wants and fears. We are the form some of the light takes. You are accurate and justified in speaking of the help we bring. To each heart. To each individual. And to the consciousness as a whole.

Fear and doubt come in in small steps. In each of these moments, you know exactly now where to send light. The name Abu Ghraib, the young farmer from Dilawar, whose suicide by burning ignited the Arab Spring. Having specific places to send light helps those areas balance and cleanse.

Your heart can be lifted by your prayers, by sending light. Especially by catching yourself when a downward feeling starts.

Hold your own heart in light as an image.
Call in the Violet Transmuting flame. Immerse yourself in it.
Align with the great I AM Presence.

You do good by stopping at the first downward twinge. You do good by this switch. Every time. You do good by asking for assistance. Every time it is given. There is more light now by this asking.

Your work to inspire is based on the daily knowledge and experience of things getting better. This is what you must continue. Be brave and strong, clear and open. Go now with peace. We love you. Hug the people. Be in peace.

~22 September 2011

Never Compare

Beautiful Angels,

Thank you for being with me tonight. I felt "less than" when I looked at what some Sacred Activists are doing all over the world. I feel foolish. What am I really doing here?

Our dear One,

You are not any of those wonderful people. Your way is so much softer. Your mother may have toughened you, but you are our Angel girl and we love the words you write. You transmit the ease that is wanted. You transmit the big, unending love. You transmit the purposeful heart. You have quite a lot of experience with unconditional love.

What can I do now? What can I do in a large group?

Breathe three big breaths in and out.

Do not even try to compare yourself with anyone. If you start to think of someone in that way, immediately send them light. This usually will get you back to your heart.

With groups, greet everyone like you do, with both your hands.
Shine.
Love.
Hold hands all together.
Call us in. We are there.

~29 September 2011

Service to Humanity

How can I best be of service to you and humanity?

Dear One,

You serve when you align with the Will of the Creator. When you offer over to us the planning or arrangement of your day's activities, you allow the purest energy to be utilized for the highest good. Every day there are hundreds of "thought-tasks" that you engage in. With our overlighting your hours, these can occur in seamless succession. Blessings smooth out energetic webs when the heart is even, centered, unhurried, and unworried. So when you give us your day, you give the entire world a blessing. Your energetic field is undisturbed; your mind field is unperturbed. This contributes to the stabilization of harmonious frequency over a broader area.

~3 October 2011

Small Things

Dear Angels,

What is your counsel today? Many situations are changing in the world.
I feel sometimes this book is too simple and too personal.

Dear Jenny love,

The small things offer sweetness to your eyes and to your life now in these rapidly changing times. The clear eyes of a child. A blackbird on the wire in front of the house. A shore bird running delightfully on thin, quick legs. A song on the radio. A tomato fresh from the garden. Small, natural things give comfort and steadiness. Looking for them, noticing them, adds to the beauty and joy in each day.

We have seen in all our workings with humans that small occurrences can be like stepping stones to a happy and steady state.

Give yourself five minutes right now and consciously notice things of beauty and natural wonder before you. Report back.

The power of this book lies in its simplicity. The truth of Angels is offered gently and accepted into consciousness. Quiet bursts of light move through the people, assisting in grounding and stabilizing. Our counsel is to relax into the truth that you know. See the beauty that is increasing.

~ 18 October 2011

Oasis of Calm

Dear Angels,

I feel like I've been avoiding writing with you, yet I know you are with me and kind to me. Now I feel better, sitting and being together. Thank you for this calming presence. Is there something you would like to say to me or all?

Precious Heart,

We like communicating with you. The essential heart is pure and easily settled. We know your heart aches too and the land is tremendously changing. You do not see the changes yet, but the subtle effects are already quite apparent. Your very world is in fluid flux. So when we visit with you, we together create an oasis of calmness. You do not feel it in your house because it is your field, but others notice it immediately. Good work is being done here. Never doubt it.

It is a grand time to be alive here on Earth! It is imperative that the heart be known and valued. This is what makes your human consciousness, the heart. Seat of compassion. Appreciator of grace. Resplendent in God's Light. The truth of your human heart. This is the journey and the start.

Let yourself drop into your heart. There is rest, peace, hope, love, and blessing.

~ 16 November 2011

Our Love Is with You

Our love is with you with such ease now. Your heart is used to loving, saying prayers, and sending blessings, thanking the water, kissing the sun. Thus you are largely open now. These quiet hours and your calm and steady openness allow for questions to us.

Do not worry about describing your first meeting with Dorie. It is the light that overlights your words. This same light transmits to each reader. There is always enough light.

The light moves in ways you cannot compare in the third dimension. You, dear One, now have more glimpses of full sight and cognition. These will increase as the light inflows you. All of your subtle training is so valuable. The culmination of your work with Dorie and all your teachers now helps as your fellow humans align in the new frequencies. Feel the light expand inside you and through you.

Always come back to your heart.

The way you feel blasted open after an orgasm—you're going to feel that with everyone. You, dear One, are going to be a model—have been a model of this already in some situations. That is why people thrive in the warm ambiance of your loving welcome, heart to heart.

Dear One, we are so glad you get this picture of you. You have known it with Dorie. Now you are it, by this vibration you carry. Your own Guardian Angels, Radiance and Serena, bless you. They bless everyone you bless.

~24 November 2011

The Greatest Service

The greatest service is to be clear and well-intentioned, rooted in the light, and then silently or aloud, call in the Angels. When you listen to the media news, when you hear a sad story, a tragedy, but also a happy event—these are all opportunities to send Angels. The way the Angels expand onto this plane, the way they have of helping, occurs when they are invited in. Your certainty establishes this in you. It inspires others. It increases the multitude of Angels.

The difficulty comes if you expect anything to go a certain way by this act of calling. It must be done with certainty and then released. Be clear in the call and then release any attachment to the outcome. Your personality may want the outcome to look a particular way. But you cannot know all the possibilities and ramifications of the call; you cannot know what is best for all concerned. You can only know that you have done your best and called your greatest allies. Then your own mind must rest, or move on to the next moment of the present.

This letting go is a big challenge, both personally and as the representative of your family's line of action and belief. Most families have the trait of holding on to anger and pain. But remembering hurt does not mitigate it. The challenge is to get off your own story, feeling sorry for yourself, and get into the glory of who you really are.

By being an Angel carrier, you have a way to lessen the sorrow that is carried out into the world. Now you can be an instrument of peace and good will. This makes you integral, makes you whole.

Love is the name given to this feeling of clear, positive support. It is so personal and so vast. It is available to everyone, anywhere in the world.

~26 November 2011

The Fragile Openness

Maybe you know it from sex
or from birth or from prayer.

That fragile sliver of time
when you know everything.

You know who you are. And
you know your place in the world.

This is really all you ever need to know.
Everything else falls from this.

It is about trusting that breath,
that instant, that touch, that glance.

Not exaggerating.
Just having it fully.

Translating Light

Dear Angels,

I love this connection. When I read the other messages, they ring so true. I feel a kind of pulling inside me. If I start the pencil, something will come. So clear. Thank you for being with me here past midnight, my dear Angels.

Dear One,

We are glad to meet you in the night. So much changes on your Earth. Now, in the night, the frequencies are more at rest, so the clear light is transmittable. That is really what we send to you: Streamers of Light. They have certain vibrations which move through your brain, activating packets of thought. You translate quickly into words and feel it if something is not correct.

Yes, this is different from the words that flow into your head as sound. In all the world of possibilities, these are not too different. But in the subtle, minutely specific area of brain function and variations in frequency vibration, these are distinctions only a few can make. At the present time, you are strengthening this receptor function.

You are a natural channel, a little ahead of the multitude. This is a skill/talent that you have and use well. Soon, most will be able to receive guidance. Still we think this gentle presentation will allay fears.

Dear One, your certainty is excellent. Like you said today, "Solid, but made of light."

~28 November 2011

My Job at This Time

What is my job at this time?

Your job, dear One, is to be happy. Be exuberant. Be full of wonder. Be positive. Be gorgeous. Be happy. Not phony, not superficial. Truly happy in the now.

Your job is to inspire hope, trust, wonder. You cannot do this falsely. Only truth shines.

Your job is to smile your beautiful smile and welcome people into the growing light.

You demonstrate someone fully legitimate in Angel communication, by your spiritual lineage. However, the real message is we are here for everyone. We have always been. Now the veils between the dimensions are very thin and diminish more every day. So we are nearer.

We want to be working with you on every project and every page. Let us help you reach more people with our love. For we only love you and we always love you. We love you.

~29 November 2011

Diminish Negativity, Increase Light

My dear Angels,

I join with you first thing as I am waking. I thank you as my last thought before falling asleep. I send prayers and blessings to people throughout the day. I immerse myself in the Violet Transmuting flame. I feel calm and easy most of the time. I feel happy. My dear Angels, please tell me how this works.

Dear and blessed One,

You are cherished and you are loved. We see your light increasing with every passing hour. This light calls to itself, attracts more light. Your cells are changing to crystalline light. Your emotions become softer. Your thoughts grow in harmony. Alignment with the higher forces increases. The process is subtle. The direction is unmistakable. The outcome is inevitable. You will be living in full consciousness as a being of light.

Diminishing negativity and increasing light operate together synergistically. It is an ongoing process. You and millions of other people are living this process now. This is thrilling to see. Your lives represent the changing life of Terra Gaia, your beautiful Earth. You are cells of her body, each day stronger in the light.

You begin to notice that doubts disappear. You have fewer questions. You live in a peaceful atmosphere of calm and appreciation. This is precisely what is needed at this "moment" in time. You live more and more in your heart. Your mind is less occupied with media, with money, with power.

You can more easily envision the coming times—the glorious coming times. Poverty will be no more. Illness will be no more. Tragedy and suffering will be gone, and rather quickly even from your memory. Your lives will be lived in ease, harmony, and contentment.

These are extraordinary times of vast change. You will be honored and revered for the courage and steadfastness you demonstrate right now. Even this most simple act of sitting with us at the start of the day is to be commended. Because you *know* we will be here, we will meet you. We will transmit the energetic codes that you translate into words as your pencil moves. By this act you demonstrate your trust. It grows along with your light. At the same time, you are grounding more light into Gaia, and that is greatly needed now. You notice the subtle perfection as small things work themselves out without you doing a thing. You are not feeling any fear; you feel relief.

Dear One, the light outside the window calls you now out into the day. Go with your heart full and your mind easy. Carry your light strongly. We will meet again later. We love you now.

~1 December 2011

Refining the Perceptual Apparatus

My beautiful Angels,

Please tell us how the increasing energies are moving in our bodies. What will we notice?

Dear One,

You are releasing old sound waves from your body electric. You are becoming a more finely tuned instrument. The first harmonies are starting to call to you. Have you not heard those small twinkling sounds in the night? The refinement of hearing is part of the refinement of your perceptual apparatus.

Incrementally you are internalizing more light. Your inner tuning mechanisms, the endocrine system and the master gland, the pituitary, are functioning more on light. They are sending signals to the outer organs in codes of light.

Your medical world sees the organs and their functioning as separate ears, eyes, nose, throat, etc. In truth, the entire perceptual system is very finely integrated. The possibility of profound comprehension can be widespread with the inflow of so much light.

You *are* functioning more and more in the light. Full of light, using light for substance and medium. Because your mind can allow it, you are comprehending in a wider frame and scale.

We love you. Trust your heart. Open your eyes. Breathe.

Let your love shine. Let your love shine. Let your love shine.
This is a quiet, cumulative growth. It is magnificence happening.
All of you. Each of you.
One by one. Together.

~2 December 2011

Take Heart

My dear Angels,

It is so pleasant to feel you whispering to me as I awaken. I feel you so close, more close and more "real" every day. My doubts are essentially gone.

Can you give us an update for the times? And can you speak about Meg? We are concerned and don't know what action to take or words to say. Thank you.

Dear One,

You are living in the light more every day. We delight in seeing the bright light streams radiating out from you. Your interactions are compassionate and loving. The calmness that you now speak about and emanate casts a soothing air around you and those you meet. It is a subtle yet stable field that people enjoy entering. It benefits all. This is good work.

The times are in immense flux. The old ways are disintegrating rapidly. It would be right before your eyes if you could see the energetic underpinnings of things—which you will see in your coming full consciousness. If your media would cover these stories, more people would be aware of the dissolving. Now some would be rocked by waves of fear at such revelations, but many would be buoyed up by the same stories. It depends on the point of view and the degree of heart opening. For when a human heart is open, the call of truth is strong. It cannot be denied or covered over. When a corrupt regime is brought down or a deceitful CEO is exposed, the vibrational benefit to all is immense.

You have a phrase, "Take heart." In your meaning it is to use your heart as a tool for strength, a place for power. And, of course, this is true. Your heart is the best and truest guide for thought and action during this phase of great transition. It is also a source of nourishment for your soul. When you live from your heart, you are naturally aligned with your soul's purpose. You fulfill this purpose in each instance of following your heart—in decisions of action and in choices of avoidance as well. Sometimes moving away from a toxic situation is the best and most suitable response. After all, your purpose is joy and expansion of happiness. Learning to leave the muck and not stay stuck is an indication of good heart connection, good learning.

The woman Meg does not have this developed heart learning. She has a mightily developed intellect, but she has not been able to connect her mind with her true heart and lives in much distress. Her resistance to following any promptings of her heart is the primary cause of her suffering at this time. Her medications could soften her resistance, but she is not making that choice. Instead she is holding with clenched teeth to the "story" she has fabricated. She replays this story, elaborating the details to bolster up her perspective. She strengthens her mind's hold on details which only serves to dig her further into her singular position. There is no way out of such crevasses. She will not let herself be swayed by another view, so entrenched is she in holding fast to her own.

It is sad to see so much talent and insight used only to uphold a false position, for there can be no true brilliance if it is unaligned with heart. This is, in fact, one of the great changes coming into your world. Mental expression without heart will be seen as dry rhetoric with no deep and lasting value.

Our advice is to send her love. Send her light. Include her in your prayers. Speak of her heart when you discuss the situation. Yes, she is delusional, but the delusion is not about abuse or the cleanliness of a room. It is about a human energy fixating on abuse rather than healing. It is about an exquisite mind untethered by connection to the heart. It is about a continual choosing to hold on rather than let go. She will not be able to remain in her mental world while humanity advances.

She has cracked many times but she has not been cracked open. Sadly, she feels more like a walled-up creature than a person whose heart is cracking open. Her peace is there if she could let it happen.

We say to her, *We are ready to comfort you. Let our love and comfort in. The love that you withhold is the pain that you carry, lifetime after lifetime.*

~5 December 2011

Assist with Transition

My dear Angels,

Please help with Theda. Please assist her. Please help me to know what to do. Please make it as smooth and free of struggle as possible. Please help her. Please help me.

Dear One,

We are with this One, who fights very hard. She only knows, as a personage, to use rage to get energized. There is no place for such attacking on the New Earth, as the vibration of anger cannot exist there.

She is so tired. She is tired of fighting too. She is feeling the call to the light. She resists out of habit, but shortly she will allow. Then she will glide toward the light and feel lighter and lighter, more and more pleasant.

She is crossing over frequently in the nights and in her bouts with stomach flu and fitful sleep. Her time of transition is near. She is fighting here but will be surprised how easy it is to pass. She will remember her soul's purpose and will not be carrying the tough stance of her personality as it has been on Earth.

It is not necessary for you to tolerate abuse. All is going as planned. Her vessel is rigid. It cannot contain the increasing light. She will snap open as she leaves. Do not fear or worry for her. Her time is near. She knows it and in her fright she may drink herself into the stupor that will set her free. We will be with her whenever she makes her transition. She is terrified but so feisty she comes over with boxing gloves on. Send her light. We are as close to her as she will allow. When you think of her, see her moving into that channel of light.

Do not fear either for her or yourself. Many await her return and they will welcome her warmly. She will quickly remember her greater connection to them and her heart will begin its expansion. This is the reason for what you call death. Another opportunity to expand the experience of life. See her moving into her light stream and send her peace and blessing.

~7 December 2011

The Dark Forces

My dear Angels,

Andrew asks, "What is the role of the dark forces at this time of transition and shift?"

Dear One,

The dark forces show you your worst self, the lowest, darkest, nastiest thoughts. Old rumors, primitive indulgences that have not been discarded. Thus every kind of hoax and display of shenanigans, no matter how blatant, is still a distraction.

Now the suggestion is to look and let go and not avoid and not indulge. As more people do this, the forces wither and die. The dark feeds on fear in every form, in every manifestation, in all of fear's many guises. Even the most natural things—birth and death—have been shrouded in fear and misdirected assistance. Both these happenings, and so many others, can be experiences as blissful, ecstatic, revelatory, but certainly not fearful.

There is fear because so many still believe it represents the true state of affairs. Once you have transcended fear, the circumstances will fall away like a robe whose strangling belt is finally loosed. When humanity transcends fear, the dark will be part of the past. In each heart must grow the knowledge that love is true, that love is just and all embracing.

Soon the dark forces will be gone from Earth. The work will be to let the remnants of them and their dark ways and tendencies leave from each being.

The stranglehold of money will be loosed. The differences between you will be significantly diminished and the fullness of your lives will become apparent. You will have so many joyful things to do, you will quickly forget the dark past and the forces that played havoc with your many lives.

The dark forces are the biggest distraction to awakening. Like the foam of debris on the wave beach, which is neither water nor sand, it is junk mixed up so as to be indecipherable as it ignobly seeks to destroy.

The very best way to spend these last days of duality is quietly being aware as the *vasanas* come up. Letting old feelings move through and out of your field is THE part of Earth's cleansing that you can do and you must do. The grace of your life has given you this perfect time and companions for this passage.

Continue to give us your day to organize. Your head is much less cluttered. It is open and spacious, so you can hear, so our words can land in you and be caught, brought down. Be easy, dear One.

Do not fret. All is in good and gracious hands. Enjoy the golden days. Fret not.

~15 December 2011

Loved and Accepted Unconditionally

My beautiful Angels,

I am full of love to be meeting with you this night, the last night of the year. Then the new year begins. My beautiful Angels, please speak about our progress and our accomplishments. We are learning to ask for more of the good, putting our attention less on faults. Thank you for your counsel and your grace.

Dear One,

This writing heals you in a profound and deep way. It heals your heart. Your destiny is beginning now as your heart heals from the thousands of lifetimes it has carried memory. Human hurt has been the collateral damage of this soul growth.

Now with the inflowing of so much light, deeper layers of some of the oldest human imprinting are rippling up through consciousness, like bubbles of air once frozen in ice. So be especially kind when you cast your eyes over this year. You have come though survival mode and you will excel in thriving mode.

We are pleased with the intimacy of our contact, as it comes across in these pages. It is so very steady and inviting. The deeper questions can come, but the grace of starting is what is portrayed here.

Our own entry into each human life means being loved and accepted unconditionally. This is what we offer and this is what we provide for the benefit of all.

These pages are for someone who has no thought of Angels. They work as reading meditations. The Angelic light vibration is in the words. It is transmission, often long before the reader is conscious of it.

These pages are for someone who knows quite a lot about spiritual work, perhaps knows about the Angels and the help we offer. They follow your entry and commitment, your deeper surrender, revealing a naked self. And so it is compelling in its simple honesty and comforting, repeating message, *We love you. We only love you.* That alone could save everyone.

If all humans knew there were Angels ready to help and that all we want is to help and love them. If every human truly felt that safety and unconditional love for one full moment, the heart chakra of the Earth would burst. So it happens individual by individual, heart by heart, page by page. In the end, everyone will know there are Angels and that their own Angels are with them in simple and miraculous ways. Once a person knows this, everything changes.

We are pleased in this messaging and in the light that is transmitted. We are pleased with the tender-hearted revelations that are shown here. It keeps alive the value of tenderness. Tender is the soil of hope.

> In this, the beginning of your new life:
> Try not to be afraid, whatever seems to be happening.
> Send light whenever you can.
> Take time to align.
> Bless everyone.

~31 December 2011

Optimism

My dear Angels,

Just sitting here like this, cold morning, sunlight bright, I feel myself happy and filled with love. I love how it feels to write with you. So I say "Hello" and "Good morning." Do you have some words for me or us? Thank you.

Dear One,

True, we do love sitting with you. The silver stream of word/thought/love is felt and subtly seen—now more and more—as we communicate. This is now part of your cellular make-up and it radiates out as you move or speak. So going to write with the good women is a special boost, because you transmit this light as well as encourage their free verbal expression.

Do you feel how the writing room brightens by the end of the session? It is because their own Angels are called in and begin to vibrate. Their high hearts are activated and the profound healings that love awakens are possible. For some of the participants, these minutes of ease, laughter, and shared exchange of words can anchor the rest of the day—or week—in positive light and hope. Optimism is the name that sparkling light assumes when it is evidenced in the eyes and heart.

Again, dear One, good work is happening here.
Go and write together. We love you.

~ 14 January 2012

Follow the Promptings of Your Heart

My beautiful Angels,

Sitting here with you—ah. Now I am breathing calmly and sense the silver light. This is what feels so wonderful. Here inside. Alone. Quiet.

Dear One,

Let yourself stretch out into the huge comfort and support of this field. Allow yourself to have it. Know you are worthy to know it and exist in it–and expand this field out.

You are following the promptings of your heart after aligning as you now do. Trust the flow of the path and allow for your latent tendencies to rise up as you release them. Trust the larger process. You are in the–one of your favorite words–interstices of the fabric as it is both unraveling and being woven together in light. So put your attention on what soothes and calms you.

Let yourself find focus in preparation. Do the vacuuming. Sweep the leaves up. Then say the blessings, hang the prayer flags, and welcome what comes into your beautiful life.

Your home and hearth and heart are true. Be kind. We love you. No censure. You are one of our frontline light carriers. Your bright and steady light and truth will be needed. You are of deep value. Let this love be you.

~16 January 2012

Working with Your Shadow

How do I work with my shadow?

Dear One,

Work with your shadow the way we work with you every day: we love you. You may not be able to start there, but your question suggests you have already acknowledged your shadow. So you have brought some awareness to something of your experience that is not in your heart of light. This something has constellated into a bundle of emotional triggers and reactions, compounded over your lifetime. Prepackaged by your lineage karma this material is precisely for you, of you, and by you. If you do not know it at all, it seems to have huge power—a wild beast. If you begin to investigate, it becomes less dense.

Your awareness, your heart focus, your intention to live with the Angels allow you to grow your light consistently and cumulatively. But your deepest work may be when you let yourself feel the immense power of your shadow. Let the wave of it fully take you and move in you as you remain steady. You may weep. You may wail. You may want to quit everything and sleep for a week, but just be steady for a few minutes right where you are. Watch those memories flash before your eyes. Catch those painful, invaluable insights and stay steady. It will pass. Let it pass out of you. Be done. And then really be done. Don't retell a story. Don't resurrect your familiar pain. It is no friend at all. Light and trust are your allies. Trust that and know we love you simply and purely.

~28 January 2012

Increasing Light

My dear Angels,

Thank you for these beautiful, smooth-flowing words. The energy is like silk. It feels so good to be alive in this. Can you speak about the times, the growing excitement? Thank you.

Dear One,

It is happening. The opening. The inflowing of light. A growing knowledge of truth. Increasing trust. More peace.

We have told you on many occasions that war is already past in your world. There will not be another war. Soon all military bases will be converted to places that support and encourage peace. Your minds and hearts are ready to envision this new world. Quietly the infilling light is raising consciousness, individually and en mass. It is happening naturally, everywhere. All humans are receiving more light. Some few of the dark do not allow any of this elixir of life. Their stories will continue to unfold, but they cannot any longer stop your growth and expansion.

When you walk out today, see the indications of increasing light in the faces of the people you meet. Speak to the one in front of you in line with kindness. This may be the first day that individual has lived with such a level of light energy. Gentle acknowledgment of light additionally increases light. Say, *How bright you look today.* This is your assignment. Enjoy playing in your light heart. We love you.

Be glad. Your instincts are right on.

We go with you out into this day of huge openness and possibility. We love you.

~3 February 2012

Change in the Air

My dear Angels,

There is so much change in the air. On so many levels I feel it. Can you speak about the upcoming times? How can we be ready?

Dear One,

The readiness is in the looking. How and what you look at now will have a lot to do with what comes next on your event horizon. Yes, the changes are happening fast now. The babe is in the birth canal. And it is the whole universe that awaits the arrival.

All of you in your best aspect—light with a human coloration. And your beautiful Mother Earth comes into position in the larger galactic world. All is happening as it should, as it must. There is no mistake about it.

Your own life path is accelerating too. This book—the strong connection with us and with Andrew—is now its own energy vortex. It is very attractive, inviting. Your tender heart has received these impulses. In your quiet mind the flow is steady and serene as it comes in. These characteristics are ideal for expansive transmission. Good spreads out from this, even now as you write, even now as you feel the silver stream again. Bless you.

Go out into the world carrying steadily and brightly your light, our overlighting Presence, and our constant support. Into the market, into the group, be the lighthouse that you are.

You see, it is not about you. You are so well placed, so well matured now, seasoned and turned in your own particular fire of grace that you are now our instrument. People can meet you under the guise of Greeter. Your openness allows them to feel welcomed into the light, knowing it or not. Each instance and each contact feeds the field. Light is fast becoming the currency of exchange. You assist in this by every interaction as well as every gesture, thought, and prayer.

You are not unique in these skills. But you are conscious and doing it broadly, easily, and regularly. Everyone benefits. That's why it feels so good. Again we say, get used to things going well for you. Get used to seeing signs and indications of the growing light. You are part of it. We love you.

~ 12 February 2012

Keeping Faith

My dear Angels,

Thank you for your guidance and support. I need to feel your wisdom and your graceful understanding. How odd it is to live in what is called the third dimension and know of your light. How do we keep our faith alive?

Dear One,

We join with you gladly on this cold morning. The day will unfold itself around your energies. So start your day with us and your alignments. Today, especially with this question in your heart, use the immense power of the Violet Transmuting flame. See the flame at your heart. See how it grows to consume you entirely in its frequency of violet light. The dross of your thinking, old habits and ways of feeling are consumed right now. You can almost hear them singe and disappear.

Such thoughts as, "How will I accomplish this task? How can I manage the logistics? What will people think?" These are chattering away inside you as remnants of yesterday and projections about this afternoon and tomorrow. But now is what is here holding us together. Now is where we love you and support you. Now is where peace lives in you.

We see the true flame of your spirit, the same as the inextinguishable flame of God in you. Now as we focus on this area, behind your breastbone, the pilot light of you burns steady and clean. Do you feel it? Circumstances may seem to turn the flame down, but no situation, adversity, or hardship can ever put out this flame. It can be adjusted higher, yes, and that is what we do with you today.

Such a steady flame. Now stronger. Now brighter. No wind can blow it out. These few moments of clear focus while you feel uncertainty allow for some fine tuning. As your Angels we can hold an etheric force field in front of and behind your heart. A quiet, unruffled force field. The flame is strong now.

Don't worry about your faith. Feel your steady flame. With each breath, notice how the flame brightens. Say, *Look now. This small flame in my heart is burning bright. My Angels are helping me. I have asked them and they hold my heart light.* The dimensional energetics are complicated. The truth of the support is easy. We love you. Your faith is our contract. We accomplish tasks and connections so you will have evidence of our presence in your life. Your heart light is your faith. When you go out today, see this flame inside your chest.

~16 February 2011

Let Love Be Real

My dear Angels,

I feel I am in the constant stream of your love. Even while the world story unfolds, I feel safe and secure. Can you please comment and inform us all. With so much love.

Dear One,

The marvelous light you saw yesterday is the truth. Your fifth-density self and life before you. Your shining, shining light.

You are amalgamating many teachings, many lifetimes, different religious practices. Through these eyes of light you see how all is One along with the unique unfolding story. Not a paradox really, but seeming.

Let love be real and alive in your life. The tendency to regret or find what is lacking, watch these old tendencies move toward the integrated position to lead, to do, to say what is called forth. With ease and grace you can trust this.

Be glad in the knowledge that you and so many more are open to the inner voice of God, which is in each of you.

We love you.

~ 10 April 2012

Acknowledge and Turn

My dear Angels,

Thank you for being with me now. Will you tell me who you are? A seed of doubt has been planted by someone. So I ask.

Do you have words for me about my mission in this transformation? I resonate with the Council of Elders. Oh my heart sings. Please tell me, my dear Angels.

Our dear One,

The singing in your heart is the clue. Yes, you have heard your call. We will tell you more as the Council informs and instructs. Your receiving and acknowledging the call is accomplished.

We knew you would know when something resonated. Now you know one more thing about free will. This is how it will occur for many, with clear and undeniable knowing.

This beautiful golden light of evening, the gloaming, is familiar and will be again your environment. Yes, soon—even in your reckoning. Now you feel the upwelling of joy. Ride each wave, grateful for the live wonder of it. Each time you can appreciate rather than blame or complain, you are transmuting energy.

Let any feelings of doubt or impulses toward criticism be acknowledged . . . and turned. You have the awareness for this. In this way, any day, any hour can be time spent well.

We are your Angels. There are many of us. Appreciate the concern behind the question and the questioner; you are in fine company, ahem. We lighten up the topic so your hearing can be clear. Archangel Michael overlights these many kinds of communication. He is not located in one dimension only. His light is our corral. We gather to be in communion with you in his grace. It is not hierarchy.

~ 16 May 2012

Lovelight Peace

My dear Angels,

I feel happier and more lifted. Wider understanding. Sometimes my heart just sings. Can you speak to this? Thank you.

You are correct, dear One. You are coming into fullness. Have been for a while. It used to be much farther away. Now it is close. The wisdom of others is contributing to your wisdom.

The process is happening beautifully in you now. No resistance. It is such a pleasure to be with you. This great emanating peace. It's not white light peace, sterile and searing. It's lovelight peace. All lovely and so excellent to behold. You.

You can't see it, but you see it in others and in the reactions to you. These are your mirrors.

~23 May 2012

The River of Light

My dear beautiful Angels,

It is a clear morning, golden light streaming over the land. What is the update for us at this precise time? Thank you.

Dear One of the open heart,

The light is part of everyone's body and awareness now. People all over the world know they are part of something whether they know precisely what it is or not. The old ways of being cannot continue as the light increases in reach and intensity. You are all part of this inoculation of light. This is what you are here to carry, in yourselves and into Gaia.

You are traveling in your night sleep to other realms that become more familiar to you. You need time to heal and refresh your spirit after another "day" in the thick third dimension. You are right in the middle of your transformation and it is proceeding well. Continue in this womb/ease. It heals your past and any anxiety in the present. You cannot push the river of light. Waiting in an open, unwavering way is excellent now.

It seems I can ask about the past and the now but I cannot seem to formulate or receive for the future?

Yes, you are not fully awake in all your centers so we do not transmit what you cannot yet receive. You are open in your heart and hearing, so the feeling of truth is what you receive and go by. All have a purpose. As you stream these flows of consciousness intertwined with light, you give this higher frequency energy an outlet here. You add to the collective light and increasing vibratory rate in this way.

Each person is adding to the increase in the best way for her or his growth at this time.

We commend you as you fall away from comparison and judgment. The best work now is exactly what you are doing: Ease, trust, refining the words on the pages. Forgiveness and acceptance and joy. Let joy wildly be. Gratitude, appreciation, kindness. These values will deepen you as they increase in your conscious awareness. So keep your attention easily and yet steadily on what is occurring in front of you and within you.

The great universe is structured by this moment-by-moment subtle awareness and its growth.

Your ease, your calm, your steady support is already of benefit to many. Let it continue, in our love, as you always are.

We love you. We always love you. Yes, you!

~29 May 2012

Loving Across Boundaries

My beautiful Angels,

I feel you loving me so much all the time. I am getting used to being in this/ knowing this/ feeling your love. So beautiful. I am so happy when I feel you. Do you have updates for me today? Thank you.

Our Dear One,

We do love you. We are glad you feel us as we have been close in your life for longer than time. Now we talk so easily and smoothly. Talk is no longer the word to use. Commune with our dear One.

Things go well overall. What seems excruciatingly slow in your third-dimensional time frame is still involving massive, minute shifts and inter-dimensional adjustments. This is so we will be ready when Source says Go. And go it will. Don't you worry. It will be grand—because we see you all connecting, loving across boundaries. These are the light crossings we love to see. They indicate your readiness. Oh yes, it will be truly wonderful.

You are living largely in fourth-density thought waves. When you get hooked in old voice and thought habits, it reminds you that you are still part of the world here and your personal inner work in the moment is evident. That which triggered you is in you in some form. Let it reveal itself for your conscious release. Let what moves through move out completely.

Feel our love for you.

~22 June 2012

Every Word Becomes Blessing

I write because the Angels call me out;
the crash and swell of ocean
roars all night in my ears.

When I wake in the glow
of the circling moon
unblinking on my small table
I empty myself of thoughts.
In a jumble of grace,
in a trance of stillness,
I write.

A steady stream flows
through arm and pencil,
moving across the page.
How many pages? How many notebooks?
I am not empty yet.
More a rolling ocean
than a standing pond.

Traced line by line
I send them out as peace flock.
As they leave my body
they soften into bird, then air,
then blessing.

Section 5

Messages for These Times (and for Sacred Activists)

A Message for Sacred Activists

The work of Sacred Activism is so vital, so important now. Sacred Activists are protected as they join, read, march, pray, and build a new world. The old is crumbling and fear could be monstrously great. But we remind you of us, the Angels, your own Guardian Angel and all the Angels of Light. Each person has this protection. Each one has his or her own source and connection through light, through the Angels. This light goes out with every powerful and exuberant word you speak out for justice, with every act you perform out of compassion for the world.

~31 July 2011

Understanding

Dear Angels,

Such a beautiful sense as I thought of all the Sacred Activists now on the planet. Do you have a message for them today?

Dear One,

Tell them the Angels are with them like a big light that is above them. All they have to do is imagine pulling on the switch, the YES switch.

Once we become real to them as lighted vehicles of God's love, they can call and send Angels often, everywhere. Everywhere their thoughts go, bring extra Angels.

Just say, *Thank you, dear Angels, for taking care of this situation.* You send light and the Angels work it out. You don't have to understand how. In fact, that's one of your biggest spells—that you can understand, or should.

The letting go, the particular surrender that comes when you give things over to the Angels is quite freeing and very empowering.

The way Sacred Activists carry their light will ignite others. To all of them, everywhere, and all the people who yearn for freedom, which grows in their hearts, we offer blessings.

These blessings go out because the mind must finally be done with the sterile desire to understand, so the heart can fully commit to the light.

~25 August 2011

For the People to Know

There are many different kinds of beings on your planet now. You will begin to know of them and eventually you will meet them. For most people, the Angels are the easiest and best way to begin.

You already have a Guardian Angel, given you when you took your first breath. Maybe when you were a child you felt your Angel, or saw it, until about the age of seven. Then, most probably someone told you not to make up stories anymore or laughed at you or worse.

But you do have a Guardian Angel and this Angel's job is to look after you and help you. Dorie used to say, *An Angel's way of feeling good, as an Angel, is to bring something into your life to help you have your dreams come true.*

All you have to do is ask. Acknowledge your Guardian Angel. Say hello. Say you'd like to see or hear your Guardian Angel more clearly. Say you're willing to receive the comfort and support of your Angel. Say thank you. Then quietly watch how it unfolds.

There are so many Angels. You never have to worry that there are not enough. If you start the practice of consciously sending light or Angels to a person or a situation or an area, profound things can happen. Sometimes you don't know what's best for a situation. So the practice of sending light sends power to the Angel of the place and helps to balance the energy. The Angels know what is needed.

Get used to the idea of asking for help and getting it. Although people who pray and people who talk with their Angels *know* it works, long-ranging deception by the dark forces has allowed millions of humans to believe there is no help or worse, that they are not worthy of help. But each person is worthy. You are worthy and your Angel is there for you, always.

The Angels are the great equalizers across all human distinctions. Everyone, regardless of age, sex, race, intelligence, power, or beauty has a Guardian Angel. Angels are the silver white light radiance between the dimensions and densities. They are the corridor of light seen when the soul leaves the body. They are equally accessible to all.

Why so few humans know this or believe this is another topic. Now is the day for letting the Angels into your life. Right now. You can only benefit. So sit quietly, right where you are, and simply begin:

Thank you, dear Angel, for being with me now.

Then speak what is in your heart.
Close with a prayer for a person or a situation.
Then bless the Earth and all sentient beings.

~1 September 2011

Message on September 11

Good morning, dear One,

It is with armloads of grace and comfort that we meet and enfold you today. It is a holy day because so many millions of people are focusing on their hearts, their loved ones, and the great meaning of life.

There are so many prayers today. We are rejoicing for the souls joined together. The sorrow the media is trying to portray is not what the real story of today is. The massive joining of hearts is the profound power of today. You feel it. You all feel the connection. Even to the hearts of the "false perpetrators."

All are humans caught in the final death throes of a giant beast—the beast of falsehood, deception, and greed. Such an event [as 9/11] will never be allowed to happen again. But the good of this huge coming together is being felt. You do not feel alone. You feel a part of a wave of love and prayer and hope for humanity. This is not what the dark forces want. But you have become too wise to their ways and they cannot dupe you into fear anymore.

This anniversary day is a turning point because good people all over the world know and feel that the power of love is stronger than fear. There will not be massive catastrophes. There will not be massive earth changes. There will be peace and today's combined-heart energies are a foretaste of that. Congratulations to you all for knowing the truth, which will be revealed. Bless you, every One.

~11 September 2011

Focus on Possibilities

Good Morning, my dear Angels,

Do you have some words for me or the people today? Thank you.

Dear One,

It is a time of ever-increasing light on your planet. We watch with happiness and anticipation as the hearts and minds of millions of people change. Sometimes the changes can be quite dramatic. Decisions to join the growing forces of light happen spontaneously. Your young people feel the upsurges in energy and in hope. To all of you we would say, *Open to receive us.*

Are there specific practices we can do to help the incoming light?

By your receptivity you are anchoring light. You assist Gaia in this way to neutralize more of the negativity that has been accumulating for so many thousands of years.

Join with us. First thing as you awaken, invite your Angels into your day. Let us help your activities and plans work out more smoothly. We can do this.

Pray/Send light. If you spend five minutes each day sending light, you will lighten your heart and immeasurably bless the lives of others.

Watch for signs of change for good. Let this be the greater focus of your attention. Focusing on the problems has never been an effective way of transforming them. Focus on possibilities. Be clear about your motives by processing everything through your heart. That is your body's truth barometer. Learn to pay attention here.

~12 September 2011

Dire Beauty

It is our pleasure and delight to be with you again. Don't ever be afraid of sitting with us. Don't ever be afraid. Period. Sounds strange to say in these times of dire beauty, but there really is nothing to fear. You are protected and now rising in consciousness—truly, every day. This beautiful Earth is rising daily in light emanations, in light consciousness. To behold it is breathtaking.

No one knows precisely when the tipping moment will be, but we all know it will be. It is inevitable and it is imminent. The light is changing and whirling. It cannot be known when it will reach everyone enough to proceed. This then is the time for purposeful prayer, focused energy, grounded living, gratitude, and patience.

This is a good time in your life. Following your heart, listening, praying, sending light, not worrying, eating well, sleeping well—continue in these practices. Avoid the media. Stay away from discussions in which you cannot positively participate. You end up feeling badly. This only lowers your vibration.

~15 September 2011

Calm and Easy

Dear Angels of my heart,

I feel so calm and easy. If I have a question, the answer comes easily or is available as we join, so I don't really have a question. Do you have a message for me or the world?

Beautiful One,

We thrill in your calmness, which moves to calm others. There is no need for worry. Events are unfolding on the inner planes, so that outer events have only their intended outcomes. Only the timing is in flow—partially because of fear-inducing news stories. We continue to encourage you to enjoy this calm and steady feeling of support, and tell it to your friends.

The world will not have very long to wait now. Your world leaders know a huge change is imminent. They do not know if they can "trust" the new energies, the new possibilities, the new people emerging. So they have one foot in the boat of the old paradigm and nearly the other foot in the boat of hope and change. Each day the populace expands in its perspective. By design the whole of the collective heart softens.

~ 17 September 2011

Waves of Lightened Love

Dear One,

The waves of lightened love are moving out through and across your planet. From the ground, through the ancient caves and dwellings of the inside-living ones, all are participating in the movement of rising consciousness. The way a pebble takes the entire pond in its embrace by the fact (act) of dropping. All of the water is moved in some way.

We see humanity emerging from under a long, thick blanket of illusion. Now your many streamers of light open out the weave. There is free space between and among the awakening ones. A luxurious expansion is felt in the deep interstices of your molecules. As the transformation/transduction from carbon-based to crystalline-based proceeds, the expansion rolls out. All is going so well and quickly now.

Be encouraged by the massive joining, the global initiatives of the people. The spark has caught. The various tinder spots will lighten up in bright flares of freedom erupting.

Can an eruption of freedom rolling across the globe be peaceful? Absolutely. Call in your guides and Angels before and during every gathering. They arrange the wave. You lend it intention. Watch with your hearts open.

Soon it will not make a difference if these events are covered by the mass media. You will all know.

~18 September 2011

Suffering

Dear Angels,

Andrew posed a question about suffering this morning. Do you want to make a reply at this time?

We appreciate Andrew's view and the power of the suffering he has seen. Part of his job is "seeing" this suffering, so attention can be placed there. His Networks of Grace are perfect channels for the good news that will be known, locally and worldwide.

In some areas, the karma of many young souls is finding its balance in short lifetimes. The choice was to be here as part of and in support of the transformation. The truth of those "losses" will be revealed when the individuals meet again.

Because Andrew has lived through catastrophic "loss" and "betrayal" he can speak to the people, many of whom only know those ways of feeling. His call to let your heart break open, even look for what breaks you open is a brave injunction. It calls for listening.

And here our missions merge. In the depth of despair is where most people spontaneously pray, cry out to Heaven for help. Now we begin to introduce the feeling of being heard. From this small entry, the wall of despair is cracked, an opening presents itself. Then it continues. We tell you the smallest experiences of hope are multiplied at this time. All good is multiplying exponentially. We watch in awe and jubilation.

Now the Angels are becoming part of your reality. Angels are the light beings who are the most familiar in name and idea to humans. Your holy books give credit to Angels for delivering messages of importance to people destined to be the leaders of great nations. It is not exactly as the holy texts describe. Most of the action is instantaneous, immanent, profoundly experiential. You do not forget when you are touched by the light of Heaven. And you do not doubt. Enlightenment is a direct experience.

20 September 2011

A Simple Peace

We want the people to know, especially the marvelous Sacred Activists whom Andrew is calling out and training—they are strong and pure of intent. We tell them that any action, a seemingly small action like a phone call or a written communication, can be powerful if they are established in an even and grounded peace. Very ardent activists may carry very simple peace inside themselves.

Allowing your Angel to participate in your life contributes directly to the increasing peace and love in the world.

As you talk with your Angel, more and more comfortably, your Angel can accomplish more for you and your dreams coming to reality.

Such a small giving—giving up will
giving up control
giving up knowing
giving up understanding—
which begins to happen naturally as you trust more in your connection to all of the truth-flowing universe through your own Angel.

We, as Angels, are not the only way this connection is realized. We are the nearest, closest, easiest route.

~3 October 2011

Closer and Closer

My dear Angels,

It seems the world is closer and closer to knowing the truth. Do you have any comment for me or for the people today?

Bless you, dear One, in your steadfast opening. We see you keeping your heart open and locked on to the Truth as it is unfolding. We see you not going into fear. We see you choosing for light and going forward in that knowing.

We see the world literally "lighting up"—turning toward light, choosing the light, choosing hope, and choosing to do it together. This is all to the good.

Now is the time to use all the tools you have in your toolkit. Now is the time to pray and love and sing the light. There is nothing to be afraid of. The huge turning that is occurring in Gaia and thus in everyone is happening with great speed. You may feel surges of energy, changes in emotions, fatigue; some will have flu-like symptoms. All of the bodies are accommodating increasing light. Be the beacon you are. There is nothing to fear.

~4 October 2011

How Can the Angels Help Humanity at This Time?

Dear One,

We help humanity now in the same ways we have endeavored to help humanity throughout the ages. We help in real ways. We are not the skimpy things fluttering around playing harps. It is sweet, in a manner of speaking, how you depict us, but we are much more substantial than those images.

Let us clarify: substantial in effect, though we are made of light. We are localized light, vibrating as one with the Creator's force. We embody and carry the Creator's unending, untarnished, potential and glorious love. We carry this love for all. Guardian Angels especially watch over, guide, support, and love their special person. In human language you might use terms like Guardian Angels, Healing Angels, Teaching Angels, Angels of countries, Angels of projects, Angels of regions or bodies of water. We can embody or represent different qualities. Like different colors all reflect the same pure light, the same light seen in different hues, we are from the same realm and Source, but we can be seen as different Angels.

You, dear One, have often remarked that the many books and articles about Angels essentially agree. Because the inspiration comes from the same quality of light, the expression, even though from different channels, will be harmonious.

Our nearness and substantiality can be of real assistance during these tumultuous times. We can do some of the "heavy lifting" of sorts, if you will call on us. Ask for assistance.

Please Angels, help me now! Angels! Help me. Whatever you say, you unhook the previous circling of your mind. You STOP. One minute of true stopping, quieting, praying can give you respite. The habit of doing it can become a tremendous strength. Having the ability to stop in an instant can be helpful during changing times. This small turn of mind is a double-sided teaching and a blessing for humanity.

So stop. After you breathe in and out a few times, after you settle, then have one true moment with your deepest self. You know exactly where that is, what that feeling is like. Just you. Just this.

That's also where your purest and closest connection with your Angel is. The quiet familiarity of this feeling can give you comfort. It can confirm in a subtle and breathtaking way that your Angel really has been with you from the start.

Knowing this, really knowing and believing this is almost all you need. Once you absolutely *know* you have an Angel (or many), you know you will be fine. It means you allow for beings beyond your standard vision, beings you cannot yet see but know. It means you can begin to see signs, indications. Shiny pennies, hummingbirds, feathers appearing out of nowhere, floating in front of you or representing themselves in ways that you know. It means you are open to the vast beauty and magic of the universe touching you and infilling your life.

Your heart, your own inner truth-meter, becomes your navigator as you move into more refined frequencies. Following what registers as truth will be your best guidance. Angels help to refine the perception. We strengthen the core belief in something more. We only love you.

Again, a very small thing, a seed: Your Angel has been right with you in a deep, soulful kinship through every instance in your life because that is your Angel's job at this time. Your Angel only loves you. Your Angel is holding the light for you now. Nothing to do with worthiness, light is the place where your true self rests.

~6 October 2011

It Is Only Getting Better

My dear Angels,

Thank you for giving me this beautiful time and space to rest and feel the expansion that is softly happening. Please say some words for me and for all of us now. Thank you.

Our lovely dear One,

We do love the stream that we come in on. The pure lovelight plasma stream, almost invisible, that you have always known. You will begin to recall and remember the light work that you did in your light incarnations. Your enthusiasm is your guide and a succinct password into the new/old realms. You are following your/our guidance perfectly. We watch as doubt lessens and just falls off. You are demonstrating how a life-living, truth-speaking light being becomes revealed.

This call to write with us becomes an instruction manual. How to live in this "reality" and advance with your body into a bigger reality. Yes, you must take your body with you, but in a much lighter form. It will be mostly energy (vibration), but there is still some mass.

Never fear. It is going so well. The light is brighter by magnitudes every day. And we needed at least seven billion souls incarnated at the same time for critical mass to be reached.

Everything is on schedule, even if we have not "time" in our awareness. We have you in our continual love energy. The grace has already descended. The light quotient is high enough. Now what will be the spark, the igniting event, the gateway?

Be of great open heart today. Smile and laugh and love.

There is only getting better to look forward to. And in that—oh, how sweet it is.
We love you.

~ 1 November 2011

Cooperation

Dear Angels,

How can we best cooperate with you?

Dear One,

This question reveals your willingness—nay, your deep desire to align with the Company of Heaven. And with that desire, with that intent firm in your heart, you come into that alignment. Each day that you state your intention to align with us, to cooperate with us, the doorway to communication is opened. You become familiar with the sense of us, our nearness, our support. You become more able to discern our promptings, our guidance for your best good and the good of all.

These promptings may lead you to conversations in which your responses are quietly influenced by us, so you say something you had not thought you were going to say, and you come into wider understanding. You may be led to take an action in support of another. You could be moved to act for us as you become a human angel.

Your cooperation is based on your trust and your surrender. As your trust grows, your surrender deepens. You will find you are in deeper communication with us and with Source. Peace comes from this. As peace grows, it widens its tender reach. For peace may seem fragile when it is new, but it is tenacious. If peace is alive in a human heart, that is our platform, our entry, our stage. We shine out through all peace-makers.

~27 January 2012

The Call of the Beloved

My beautiful Angels,

Thank you for being here. The room softly shimmers. I know it is not the fog leaking in. Thank you.

Can you help in this question of message and presentation?
Andrew powerfully and forcefully rouses people to open to their roles as Sacred Activists.
Is there another way? He asks about "the exact right attitude." Do you have advice for him?

Dear One,

The static you had in wording the question is precisely to the point. Does Andrew rouse the people by his own explosive desire for the world to be saved? Does he start the breaking open process by his modeling the dignity and beauty of dancing with the wild Divine? His charisma comes in part because She has taken him and is using him. It is irresistible.

But to crack the people open now, to call them out? What is the method now? The light of consciousness is dawning and the needs of the heart are great. Most everything you have known as humans living life on earth is changing. The subtle energetic changes precede the later ones that will show on the physical. They will happen and they are happening, but you do not generally see them yet. Still, the underpinnings of your existence are changing. Everywhere people are longing for a deeper life.

You have the opportunity to offer energetic hope. Andrew has named it. He has the possibility, the drive, and the stamina to walk that hope around. Tell the people of our unwavering protection and support. The call from the Beloved is the Earth's call. She is calling humanity to receive her and to honor her as the New Earth.

When he recites, *Rise up now. Come away*, it is his own call from the Beloved to leave the ash of despair or driven duty. To break out into a life lived moment by moment with the Beloved.

The call of Mother Earth in concert with the immense inflowing light—this is for everyone. It is this rise in consciousness that he can effect. Andrew demonstrates in perfect congruent blazing how to answer the call and live.

The entry of the invisibles and the Company of Light into his consciousness and vocabulary are infusing his whole system with an additional stream of knowing. This project, catching our love in daily doses, accomplishes a subtle turning. It is happening now.

~ 17 February 2012

SECTION 6

Practices: How to Bring the Angels Into Every Part of Your Life

Wondrous Courage
Diving Deep

I surrender, right here, down into a core of peace.
Like a clear stream, it moves but is always itself.
And like that, I move through the world,
A tangle of old habits and new roads,
Of vain strivings and pure release.

I know my soul by its excitement, its push up
Through me, so that I must express it.

Old images of faces around an ancient fire.
Elders revered, wisdom carried out
From the hidden basement of awareness
Into the valley of wild abandon.

I had thought abandonment was no longer the problem.
Now I see we have all been abandoned
By the elders, the waters, the four-leggeds, the trees.
And yet we are all continually saved by them.

Wisdom is available in this dance.
One step, one clap, one heartbeat.
To this I surrender.

I remember, I forget, I surrender.
I remember, I forget, I surrender.
This is how to grow in grace and kindness.

Dorie's Introduction to the Angels

Dorie used these words to introduce people to the Angels. Imagine her soft voice speaking to you.

I'd like to tell you about Angels.
You have a Guardian Angel, and it's very, very real and is a fact of life.

Most people don't really know about Angels, because they are invisible. There are lots of facts in our lives which are invisible and we never even question them. Not the least bit. The most important of all the invisible things is the air we breathe. Without air, we couldn't even live. And yet it is invisible. When the wind blows, we can see things happening. We don't see the wind. Another very interesting power is gravity. Without gravity, we would just fly off the earth and nothing would grow the same way. Nothing would be the same without gravity, but it is invisible.

One more I can really think about is magnetic power. The magnetic power is all around the whole earth. Magnetism is in our bodies, but we can't see it. We can only see what it does. It's the same with Angels. Mostly we don't see them, but we do see things happening once we get acquainted with our own Angel.

Your Angel, right this moment, is beside you. It probably looks like colored light. Angels let you know when they are near you by perhaps a little flash of light or the tinkle of a bell. You might smell perfume. Very simple little things happen, and after a while you begin to know it's a signal from your Angel. And this signal says, *Here I am.* Your Angel was given to you when you born and will be with you always. Every person has an Angel, and mostly they don't know about it. But you know about your Angel right now.

Just very quietly, breathe easily and gently. You begin to feel comforted. You feel protected. You feel an inner knowing that a very important thing is happening within you right now. You are opening your heart to your Angel's love. Angels are lovers, companions, guardians. They are messengers from God. The word "angel" means messenger. When God has a message for you, the Angel brings it to you, and suddenly you feel an urging to phone someone, to read a certain book, to do something, to go some place. And you will find, when you follow those urgings, that something magic happens. Sometimes you meet someone that you've wanted to meet and you didn't know where they were. Sometimes you need help. You will be led to the place where the help is waiting for you.

Angels are healers. They heal relationships, situations, your home, your financial problems. Whatever the problem, your Angel will be a healer for you in the situation. If, by any chance, someone is angry with you, just speak to your Angel. *Dear Angel, please let my friend know that truly all I want is that we love one another. Let my friend know how important loving each other is.* Your Angel will go and touch the heart of your friend. You can feel what happens. The anger and the upset have melted. When you meet your friend again, you just have the most wonderful feeling of *I'm so glad to be with you.* It's as if it's the dawning of a wonderful, new day. Between you is the feeling of the fresh morning air.

There are wonderful stories of Angel happenings and I'd like to tell you a little bit about Angel healings. If you were here with me, you would notice what is happening. I'm going to reach out to you now. I put my hands in yours and I ask the Angel to find any place within you where you would like help. There begins to be a current of loving, vital energy flow into you now. Wherever the hurt has been, the current of healing will touch you and melt whatever needs to melt. Your Angel is so protective now, putting its hands over your heart. The Angel is allowing the healing love to heal you.

Sometimes the Angels will go to a far distant city or a country and the Angel will take the healing power and use it to help anyone who has asked. Children especially are aware of their Angels. The children can see the Angel when it comes.

When you go to bed at night, or in the day, or any time, the Angel puts its wings around you. You are cradled in this lovely softness. It is the most wonderful feeling to feel yourself cradled by Angel wings. When you first hear this, it sounds impossible. But with God, all things are possible. The impossible becomes possible. So your Angel can come and cradle you as you are falling asleep. Angels can take away your fears, because with your Angel to trust, you need not fear. As you begin every day to talk with your Angel, every day it will become more real to you. Every day it becomes truly your intimate companion. You find that all day you are saying, *Dear Angel, thank you for being with me. Dear Angel, thank you for your strength in me. Most of all, thank you for your love in me.*

When you feel the Angel's love in you, something truly happens. You feel as if you are living in another world. You find that you are looking through Angel eyes at the world, which only means you are looking at the spirits of people, of happenings, of things. As you look through these eyes, you are also looking at everything with love. When you look outside, everything is so beautiful, and you say, *Thank you, Angel, for all this beauty.* The beauty could be a bird or a flower or a bug or a neighbor walking down the street. Maybe you're being very thankful that you have eyes to see the beauty. You feel it's another world. Your whole life begins to change. You know if anything happens unexpectedly the Angel is right beside you to take care of everything.

I have a little angel—it's only a little, tiny figure of a Christmas Angel—it's standing on the dashboard in my car, just to remind me. Every time I get in the car, *Thank you, dear Angel, for protecting me all the time. Dear Angel, thank you that you are here. You are in the car. You are beside me.* The little angel just reminds me to say thank you.

If anyone is in need of help, I send my Angel. I only do it so simply: *Dear Angel, please go now to the hospital. Go and see Mary. Put your hands in hers and let her feel your Angel peace. Let her feel the joy of your presence. Let her feel freedom from pain, freedom from concern. Dear Angel, protect her with your wings.* That's a very simple thing to do. The Angels are filled with invisible power. Sometimes someone will be sent home the next day. Then we all smile and say, "Well, it must have been the Angels." And we know deep inside it was the Angels.

So in your life it is your Angel that from now on will care for you. You need never be lonely or ever alone. You will talk with your Angel. You will share all kinds of poetry and music. *Dear Angel, thank you for this lovely music. Thank you, dear Angel, that you are part of this great host of Angels who cover all the world. Thank you, Angel, that when I talk with you, the message goes out across all the world. A message that says, 'Love is invisible. Love is powerful. Love is joy and helping and laughter.'* Your whole day now will be filled with things and happenings which your Angel brings to you. *Dear Angels, bless us all.*

~*Dorie D'Angelo, transcription of audiotape, 1983.*

Strengthening the Connection

What is something people can do every day to strengthen their connection to their Angel?

A beautiful simple question. It comes from the place where a person does not yet believe he or she really has an Angel. We know many people may be quietly nodding their heads in agreement. How wonderful, then, that you are reading these words. Just such a small interest or curiosity is what is needed.

So you, as an intelligent, open-minded, heart-aware person might say, *I would like to know my own Guardian Angel.* By stating this intention, aloud or inside, you give your Angel permission to enter more closely into your life.

Now you begin with one minute a day, as you are brushing your teeth or shaving, or even better, before you start your active day. For one minute thank your Angel for help in the things of the day.

> *Thank you for helping me say the right words when I speak to my boss at the meeting today.*
> *Thank you for a safe and smooth drive to work.*
> *Thank you for help in studying for my exams.*
> *Thank you for lessening the anxiety I feel.*
> *Thank you for my good health.*
> *Thank you for good communication with my friend.*

These are good ways to use us. Ask for help. Rely on our support. Know that we will be there. As you discern our influence, your confidence increases.

State Your Intent Daily

Use clear words to join with us. Do this first thing every morning, before you are even fully conscious, before you open your eyes. You may hold your hands in prayer or on your heart if it adds to your focus.

Dear Angels, I give the organization of my day over to you.
My intent is to align with the Will of Creator and the Divine Plan for my life.
I align with the Divine Plan for the Earth and all who live on her.

I align with the great I AM Presence.
I immerse myself in the Violet Transmuting flame.

This will set the focus for the day and fill it with the power of love.

Dorie Says

Just love everybody.
Let your heart be open
and let the lovely Angels flow through you.
They are ever ready.
Your thought brings them into focus for this movement.
It is a service that you offer
to think the Angels will always flow through you.
Then they will.

Can you know more?

Putting your attention on the tips of your fingers
opens the channels for the light to flow.
At each tip is an energy doorway.
Imagine the Angels starting to flow from your fingers and hands.
This is a wonderful way to bring them right here into your body.
A lively energy sustains your body.

It is not up to you to judge.
Everyone can benefit from your light of Angels.
Whether you say something or not,
it makes no difference.

* * * * *

You can increase your sensitivity to feeling and sending light.
Pull a hair from your head.
Place it in the middle of a bible.
Turn one page over it and close your eyes.
Slowly move your fingertips across the page.
Can you feel the contours of the hair?
Each day turn another page over it.
You might get so that you could feel
a single hair through quite a lot of pages.

Sending Light

It is a beautiful practice to send light. Your sight expands when you send light. You will begin to feel it in your palms when you send light. Then you might see the soft light around that person's heart. It is not your business what happens, whether the person receives it or not. Only send the light.

As your field expands you will see more light activation. The light draws to itself adamantine particles of light. So light attracts more light.

The news is in the sending. The power of the sending is a mystery to explore. As the sender, you are intermingling with, being bathed in glorious, holy, familiar light.

Sending light to people is easy. See the Angels with them. Don't make it complicated. Just send light. It is in the sending of Angels that the power manifests.

Silence & Focus & Location (end point) make the light streams fly. The power multiplies, amplifies, by the act of sending.

You may have been taught that Light and Love are different. At a certain level it is empowering to discern differences. Much glory is experienced with refined perception. But now, the Light and the Angels are the same. Love = Light = Angels, who are God's pure messengers. God's personal gift.

The beautiful Nowness of this Light; just click into it and it is there, extant.
The whole field in place, as it has always been.

One-Minute Practice

One minute, any one minute when you will not be disturbed. You could be driving or washing the dishes, sorting laundry, riding the train, or in an elevator. It doesn't matter. The idea is to be able to do it *any* minute. Airports, laundromats, car washes, restaurants.

So here you are. Your one minute. Doesn't matter if you believe. Just do it.

Say, *I send light to* ________.
Your mother, your father, your partner, your kids, anybody who comes to mind. Just think the name. Any image, a song, people who sing them, events, gatherings. You can let your mind romp and still send light.

Send light to everyone. Send light to everything. You can name all the creatures you love, those you see and those you think of. You can observe the associations and still send light. Every category is endless. There is no wrong way to do this. Just keep it going for one minute, *I send light to* ________.

You can do this many times a day. It clears everything in the middle of the mind. Confusion is gone.

This is a stopping technique. A time out.
When you become aware that you are going toward fear, or criticism, or anger, you can stop. If you have material that is coming up to consciousness, it means it is coming up to the light.

It is an act of bravery to stay steadfast while an old terror comes to bite you. But in these single human moments, you are acting as a microcosm for the whole. You step forward by not succumbing to old triggers. You add tremendous power and light to the growing Earth by each moment of practice.

Longer Practice

Sometimes the urge or the opportunity for longer practice arises: running, bicycling, a boring speaker, waiting in line. These can allow an extended dip into light work.

By sending light you activate the light grid that surrounds the Earth. You amplify light by sending it. Areas, people, events can be assisted. Small, quiet blessings. It feels wonderful.

Once the Yes of your body is felt, you will enjoy the quiet solitude of sending light to all the people you can surprisingly remember—your elementary school teacher, your Scout troop or sports league, a friend you have not spoken to in decades.

When you freely let your mind associate, you allow memories to come forth in a release of old energy. Yes, there may be emotion, but the instruction here, for a certain number of minutes, is to send light. That is all you do.

Many people do not consciously know their connection. This small practice will open them simply and profoundly.

Simple Heart Practice

A simple practice that gives great pleasure.

I swim laps in a near-by pool, outdoors. One mile each session. That's thirty-six laps. I complete my warm-ups by doing four lengths of just dolphin kicks. Using a snorkel and goggles, my face is in the water, watching the sun shadows dance on the pool bottom. I used to just let my arms slide along, easy and relaxed, while I dolphin-kicked back and forth. Now I do the kicks while holding my hands in front of my high heart, in prayer.

I thank my Angels, Radiance and Serena, for being with me and I really feel them, right there in the water. I thank the Angels of all the people swimming there for being with them, and the people who run the pool facility. Then I let my mind go. I name my neighbors, my family, the kids traveling and the ones starting back to school. I name each one and catch an instantaneous flash of their face or essence.

Maybe I read an article on the web or heard a piece of news. Any image or name is a place to bless. Whole neighborhoods, whole countries, institutions, individuals, creatures—any being is a worthy place to send your heart blessings.

I let my mind jump and skip and freely associate, all the while consciously sending prayers and light blessings. I enjoy the circles my mind makes, to loop around and bless everyone, separately and in groups.

The people in the pool might think I am doing arm exercises, but it is my heart that feels the expansion.

Water Prayer Practice

I started calling in my Angels as I swim. They send very clear signals through the water. When I call them I immediately feel a huge charge of light directly into my heart from the back.

I am filled with high-frequency light and undifferentiated love and appreciation. I send this out to all the people in the pool. Sometimes I see the light streaming and reaching their arms and legs, but mainly the hearts of the people swimming. Water is a wonderful medium through which to send light.

Dr. Masaru Emoto says all water is connected. Every time I swim, I bless all the water, all the world's water, the rivers and streams, inlets, estuaries, outer banks, oceans, bays, and every waterway. Love and gratitude structure the water with this most positive vibration.

Forgiveness Practice

Forgiveness means releasing regret, sadness, hurt, fear, guilt, blame, resentment, and the desire for revenge. You will be amazed how good it feels, even if you don't, at first, believe a word you are saying. Just read the words aloud and notice where your voice catches. Be easy. This is the nature of forgiveness.

I am willing to forgive.

I give myself permission to let go.

I forgive myself for everything.

I forgive everyone for everything.

Forgiveness is a gift I now give to myself and those around me.

I easily forgive all those who need forgiving and I forgive myself.

The more resentment I release the more love I have to express.

I forgive myself for irritation.

I forgive myself for judgment.

I forgive myself for impatience.

I forgive myself for anger.

I forgive myself for fear.

I forgive myself for love I could not give or love I could not receive.

I forgive myself for holding back on my own creativity.

It feels good to forgive.

Forgiving makes me feel light and free.

I am at peace.

Personal Energy Practice

Every individual is transmitting energy. Now you begin to learn to pay attention. Once you are aware of your ability to send energy, you multiply your power for good.

Begin by holding your hands in front of you about six inches apart, palms facing each other. If it helps to focus and perceive better with your eyes closed, you can do that. Move your hands easily and slowly toward each other.

After a few seconds you will notice a subtle feeling of resistance between your palms. This is your own energy field feeling itself. Imagine it as a ball of energy, which you can enlarge.

With your attention, you can increase the power. You may feel your hands getting warmer. You may feel buzzing or tingling. When you push into the ball of energy it gets stronger and more compact.

Now you can use this energy. Move your hands over your body. Any area of pain or soreness can be eased with this energy. Hold one hand in front and one behind your knee. Same for your neck or throat. Your hands on your closed eyes feels wonderful.

Once you feel comfortable with your own energy field, you can send energy to others. Other places, other people, animals—all can benefit. You may not know the effects, but you will feel stronger and clearer in the sending.

When We Gather Together, the Angels Come

When a group of people are gathered together to hold an Angel Circle, the Angels come. The Angels will guide the talk, the silence, and the flow.

This, in itself, is a great boon. You need not be afraid that you cannot do it. You are not doing it; the Angels are guiding and directing you as well as every other member of the group. The people have come to be in the great presence of Angels. With that as a purpose, the Angels of each one, as well as the Angel of the newly formed group, will guide the group and the flow. Not to worry; never to worry.

People who come together frequently, who are used to being together regularly, can derive great benefit from calling in the Angels at the start of the gathering or their workday. Only one person need call them for the group to be overlit.

If appropriate, join hands and share one moment of quiet. Breathe in and out three times. Feel your feet firm and steady on the ground. You might say out loud, *Thank you, dear Angels, for being with us here today. Help us to speak from our hearts and listen with our hearts. We especially thank you for your support and guidance on* _________ (the topic or issue). *Help us to come into harmony as we talk and work together.*

A communal meal is also a natural place to join. You can ask the Angels to be as sentinels of light in the corners of the room. You can do this whenever you enter a concert hall, a stage, or a classroom. Any teaching space is enhanced if the Angels are invited in.

If you have words of your own, your own invocation, expressed from your quiet and sincere heart, that is excellent. You cannot go wrong when you call the Angels in. Your Angels love you. Your Angels support you as all your endeavors become filled with divine light.

A Healing with Your Angels

Start in a simple way. Sit. Take a few big breaths in and out. Now say the words, just as Dorie did.

Now we join, with the great healing power of the universe. We join with our own Guardian Angels, we join with the Angels of Healing.

Thank you for coming. Today we would like to have. . . .
Now say, very clearly and directly, specifically what you would like to have happen. This is not about anybody else. Speak your own heart's wish. Say the outcome. What does it look like? How would it feel? *(ex., Thank you for easing the pain in my shoulder. Thank you for helping my digestive system to function smoothly.)*

Be grateful for what you have right now.
Thank you for this moment to sit with you and receive your love and grace and healing.
Thank you for taking away any fear. Thank you for filling my heart with love, with gratitude, with happiness.

I feel your arms so tenderly around me. I feel the comfort. I take this and receive this deeply inside of me. I feel the tension melting away. A feeling of ease moves through me. From the top of my head it flows like warm silver light. It flows down the back of my neck and across my shoulders, wrapping them in a soft light.

The light moves down to the level of my heart. My heart is encircled now in your loving light. With every breath, with every heartbeat I feel more ease and comfort. My heart is now suffused in soft light. This light penetrates every cell of my heart, every fiber and every corpuscle. In this light, memories may come up to be released. Areas of pain and shadow let themselves be bathed in this healing light. I feel easier. I feel softer. I feel more peace.

This light moves down into the organs of my body. I see the organs drinking in the light. Each organ takes in the light. Every part of my digestive system receives light. All the glands, the nerves, the muscles in whatever way I picture them—they all receive this glowing, healing light.

My stomach, my liver, my gall bladder, the organs of reproduction, the path of elimination, my skin, my bones, my legs, my knees, my feet, my toes. Every part of my body takes in and receives light.

Areas of soreness or pain or tension let go their hold. A new ease is known. A new sense of calm and safety. I trust this feeling inside me now. I let the light move in and through me. I can imagine that my own Guardian Angel is directing this light in exactly the best way for my comfort and healing at this time. I know I can call on my Guardian Angel whenever I want. Thank you. Thank you.

You can record yourself reading the words. Then your own voice will guide you deeply into your healing.

Beacons of Light

Imagine yourself with your own Angel right there with you. See yourselves together as great beacons of light. See the light entirely moving through you, filling every part of you. Then see it moving outward to touch the people around you.

It is natural to give of your light to others. It is simple and clears your energy and your mind. And it makes a difference. Imagine thousands of people all doing the same thing and you have a powerful source of light that is lifting humanity.

* * * * *

Unconditional love is not an emotion like human love. Unconditional love is the highest frequency of light. It is the creative force of the universe. It activates your healing, your creativity, and your transformation when you integrate this high frequency light into your consciousness.

Unconditional love is also the bonding force of the universe. It creates a sense of unity consciousness, Oneness, for those who embrace it.

Global Practice

When you are in your home, quiet for a moment, or undisturbed in nature, begin to see yourself as a place of light. Maybe you imagine your whole body filled with light. Maybe you imagine a great column of light. You might start as a bright spark of light. You exist in the light of your own being, as one who holds blessings in your heart.

As you get comfortable in this imagining, begin to enlarge your sphere of influence. If you are using a column of light, see it stretch high above you. Or if a spark of light, see it fly up to the tops of the trees, above the telephone wires, to the topmost buildings.

Now use your wider imagination as you look around. Not just your house, you can begin to see your neighborhood, that major road, the next town, the interstate. You might see the curve of a river, the forest canopy, or the ocean's sparkling blue.

Enlarge your view again. After a while (and with the aid of Google Earth for practice) you can increase your purview to include your whole county. Then your state. Your country. Eventually you can hold your imagining wide enough to see the curvature of the Earth.

This is the size of your energetic blessing. Now you can hold millions of people within your heart. From here, let your prayers, praise, love, and gratitude flow.

Great I AM Presence Practice

Invoke the great I AM Presence, even if you don't know what that means. Just say the words. Because every time you consciously say the words I AM, you are fulfilling the true destiny of the words. You are invoking God as Presence in that moment. It is a holy act.

I align with the great I AM Presence.

Put your thumb and middle finger together. That is the size of your prana tube. It is part of the sacred geometry of your body that your prana tube is exactly that dimension. Everyone's is the right size and in position. Everyone has the capacity to receive and translate light.

From up above your head, imagine this tube of light flowing into you, entering where the fontanel, the soft spot was, your crown chakra. The tube of light runs down your core, along your spine. You could feel the light moving exquisitely and slowly, reaching and flooding each area, each chakra, each organ system. Or you might feel it like a rush of silver, straight down in a flash. It moves through your whole body, out through the root chakra, down into the ground.

Send this shoot of light down into the Mother, down, down into Her core. Latch it or fasten it or blend it. Anchor it or meld with Her core. Find your image of connection so you feel you truly are connected.

Now the further magic. As soon as you are connected to Earth, the Heart of Gaia, this shoot of light comes back up through your core, up through your crown, and showers out to all the atmosphere around you. You are in your vortex of creation.

I immerse myself in the Violet Transmuting flame.

Saint Germaine is keeper of the I AM and closely associated with the Violet Transmuting flame. Imagine the color of French violets, lupine, or iris. A clear, deep violet, with a touch of pink and a hint of silver. These violet flames burn everything that is not of love.

Imagine a bonfire of violet flames. You are in the center of it. When you immerse yourself in the Violet Transmuting flame, it burns up everything unwanted or old, but it does not burn you. It transmutes energy back to pure prana. It feels thrilling, cool, and pleasant.

It is a transformation of immense power when you do these things:

Center and align with the great I AM Presence,
Send light through your prana tube and anchor it to the Heart of Gaia,
Received back the surge of light thought your core, up and out the top of your head,
Immerse yourself in the Violet transmuting flame.

By this basic practice you bless Gaia, yourself, and the world around you.
The more you do it, the more potent it becomes.

In this way you have transmuted the latent karmas and accumulations of the day.
You are strengthened in your core of light as you become a fountain of light.

Affirmations: Creating the Atmosphere So the Angels Can Come

Spend some time each day saying positive messages to your self, either silently or out loud. Feel them as you say them. These are some suggestions. I hope you will write your own as well.

In unusual situations, in airports, in traffic, waiting in line, or when I am dealing with difficult people or in challenging circumstances, I find it of great help to say or think some of these words.

I desire to know you, my Angels.
Please help me to connect with you, in complete alignment with the Divine Plan.

My Angels make their presence known to me in ways that are comfortable and easy.

I give the organization of my day over to my Angels.

Thank you, Angels, for another day of loving.

I fill myself up with the light you are sending me.
May this Light align my being with Divine Intelligence.

I align with the Will of the Creator.

I align with the Divine Plan for my life.

I align with the great I AM Presence. I immerse myself in the Violet Transmuting flame.

I allow my body to receive and gracefully integrate these frequencies to assist my spiritual evolution.

I receive and express the Creator's Love. I am loved.

I forgive naturally and easily. I give and receive love freely.

My heart is full.
I have so much to be grateful for.

I am at peace.

I am surrounded with the Light of your protection.

I am filled with the Light of your Love.

I breathe in light with every inhalation and breathe out love with every exhalation.

I align with my Source. I anchor and embody Divine Presence on Earth.

Section 7

Final Inspiration

The Space Around Me Breathes

The ocean breathes me open
on a dark December dawn.

This light is many kinds of grey,
variations moving through me
like notes on a scale of sky.

Three brown pelicans, gliding
close to the edge of foam,
take me on their skim.

Silver fish bob and churn
in the swirling waves, slipping
out to thin lines of shine.

A new bird, some mix of mallard
and dark goose, has lived for a week now
in the estuary that feeds the larger water.

I am reminded that all creatures
live in the perfect & unutterable
balance of air and water and light.

In these last short days I find
another kind of light to feed me
as the night hours lengthen
and the sun sets lower,
more thinly
in the western sky.

God's Footprint on the Land

1.
The bricks of the Church came later
after the stone was rolled away
and the radiant emptiness revealed.
At first it was just space and light.
Now, after more than two centuries,
it is a small stone cave, within a cavernous
church in Old Jerusalem.

I had been before in these bare chambers,
my hand had touched the ochre stones.
Drawn to the place without knowing,
I entered the cool recess of the tomb alone.
Wax and burning candles covered an altar
as near as my outstretched arm.
Incense and prayers of fifty million pilgrims
thick and sweet in the hushed ancient air.

Then time stopped.

In the hollow within the altar
a great glow roared across the space.
Incredible, undeniable brightness
in front of me, behind my eyes—
what Saul saw.
The road to Damascus, hot and dusty.
I am nowhere; there is only blazing.

2.
When I return in the new century
the city is more modern around it,
but in those cobbled streets and passageways
the old lives fully with the present.
Handkerchief clipped to my head, I bow,
once again enter the small empty tomb.
Standing for a moment in the stillness,
Voice of Gold rolls over me unbidden.
Bigger than an ocean and softer,

a waterfall of golden sound pours over me:
I am with you my child.

The words and the light are the same.
Same bright truth, same shining.
It is my own heart blazing.
God glorifies me and annihilates me
in that small cave room.

3.
In a restaurant on the Mall,
I speak softly about Jerusalem to my two friends.
The great holy light comes again in the telling:
Church of the Holy Sepulchre;
my heart pouring out light
and Lord Christ, his hands, bright before us.
The whole room warm and golden above our forks and knives.

4.
When I think of that small cave
and wash my eyes over anything here
it is sprinkled with stars.
Long-term fears dry up and scatter
like dust in the wind.
Close-up things are covered in a soft light.

Coming home tonight, back to my little cottage,
everything is laden with light, thick with light
like the Milky Way in my living room.
The rug, the door of the fireplace box,
the red bricks. Entire room alit,
everything alive and bouncing off radiance.

It is still that same moment.
I know there is no death.

So much glory in the hollow of a footprint.
Fly up the luminous fishes, the loaves, the wine.
Come feed your deepest hunger. Caretake your precious Soul.
O awaken, heart, to the wild impossible light.

Saved

I see it when I prepare food.
Chopping vegetables or pouring out grains of rice
I see how I watch the pieces that get left out
or the grains that fall away from the pot.
I always pick them up,
taking the extra effort to wash them again
if they've landed on the floor or the counter top.
I put them back in the pan or the soup.
And always I think of the biblical story:
The great Lord God talking
about who will live and who will die
in Sodom and Gomorrah.

Abraham asks, "If I can find fifty righteous people,
will you destroy the whole city?"
Then finally coming down to
"What about one good person—
will you destroy the whole place if I can find one good soul?"

I always think of that and save the grain of rice.
Thinking this one has come so far, grown with all the others,
come finally to my kitchen, in my hand,
and now I have dropped it. So I rescue the one grain or bean.

Thinking always if someone saw me,
I would also be rescued.

When I am reminded
who I truly am—
    I am the cook.
    I am the water.
    I am the pot.
    I am the bean
      finally seen and savored.

Done

Done.
The big job is done.
Bringing in the Angels. We took it on and we did it.
That is not a boast. But I had been so concerned that it wasn't enough,
all these years and me wearing the cloak, carrying the mantle.
I saw it again so clearly today—
the long cloak, the same blue that Dorie was,
the day of her Celebration of Life in Carmel.
Today it wore me.
We wore it together.
Moving the landscape of the Angels.
Pulling along the whole scenery like a thick carpet of wonder
heavy with Presence
coming slowly over the land.
I though it would come from above.
But it overlaps the globe
on earth, on the ground.
All the same.
The ribbons of the great cloak of the Angels
got loosened today.
Dorie said, "It is done.
Not finished, but complete for you, my dear."
She gave me the pure heart love.

Big me walking
Earth Gloria Girl
La Primavera
all birds and buzzing light.
Hoisting along this thick carpet of landscape
which happens to be full of sparkling things.
Life forms
in their precious beginnings.

The root of an amaryllis
and its strong green stalk
shoot straight up
in me as I speak.

The tip grows through my chest,
tormenting
my old self.

She cannot breathe there anymore.
The flower chamber is so hot and wet.
Confusion like phlegm coughs up,
breaking up boundaries.

A maroon velvet ribbon
tied the landscape to my breast.
It caught at my throat.
Now that ribbon is loosed.
Dorie said the work is done.
Angels have arrived at a certain level of thickness
here on the planet
and we will be saved.

Surrogate mother
Angel heart,
Dorie fed me of it
daily, and I supped well.
I drank her pure love in.
Kept it uncontaminated.
Kindled with kindness,
the joy of sea beaches,
the waves and the dolphins.

Now like the perfectly heavy
buds of rare orchids
that separate their top sepals
from their green undercoats,
we burst out
dangling wings of fire.
Within warming sunlight
and perfect photon minutes
we all open up.

What a song of praise and blessing.

CPSIA information can be obtained
at www.ICGtesting.com
Printed in the USA
BVHW011251150821
614465BV00014B/1044